T0325477

# MASTERING
# THE AUSTRALIAN
# HOUSING MARKET

# MASTERING THE AUSTRALIAN HOUSING MARKET

JOHN LINDEMAN

Wrightbooks

First published 2011 by Wrightbooks
an imprint of John Wiley & Sons Australia, Ltd
42 McDougall Street, Milton Qld 4064
Office also in Melbourne

Typeset in ITC Giovanni 11/15pt

© John Lindeman 2011

The moral rights of the author have been asserted

National Library of Australia Cataloguing-in-Publication data:

| | |
|---|---|
| Author: | Lindeman, John. |
| Title: | Mastering the Australian housing market / John Lindeman. |
| ISBN: | 9781742468525 (pbk.) |
| Subjects: | Real estate investment — Australia.<br>Real estate business — Australia. |
| Dewey Number: | 332.6324994 |

All rights reserved. Except as permitted under the *Australian Copyright Act 1968* (for example, a fair dealing for the purposes of study, research, criticism or review), no part of this book may be reproduced, stored in a retrieval system, communicated or transmitted in any form or by any means without prior written permission. All enquiries should be made to the publisher at the address above.

Cover design by Design by Committee

All Microsoft Excel screenshots reprinted by permission from Microsoft Corporation.

Cover image © xJJx, used under licence from Shutterstock.

Printed in the United States by Quad/Graphics

10 9 8 7 6 5 4 3 2 1

**Disclaimer**
The material in this publication is of the nature of general comment only, and does not represent professional advice. It is not intended to provide specific guidance for particular circumstances and it should not be relied on as the basis for any decision to take action or not take action on any matter which it covers. Readers should obtain professional advice where appropriate, before making any such decision. To the maximum extent permitted by law, the author and publisher disclaim all responsibility and liability to any person, arising directly or indirectly from any person taking or not taking action based upon the information in this publication.

# Contents

*To Carolyn*

# About the author

No-one knows the needs of housing investors better or understands the housing market more thoroughly than John Lindeman. John has more than 10 years' experience researching the nature and dynamics of the Australian housing market at the Australian Bureau of Statistics. He has also spent five years as head of research at Residex, Australia's oldest and leading property information provider, where he has managed the development and dissemination of residential housing information and research services to government at all levels, major banks and non-bank lenders, developers, finance and investment advisers, institutional investors, private housing investors and the media.

His knowledge of and expertise in the housing market is enriched by more than 30 years' experience as a successful property investor. John is a recognised authority on the housing market, and his presentations and commentaries are highly sought after.

# Introduction

Buying property is not something most people do without a great deal of thought and research. The housing market can appear to be such a complex and unwieldy beast that investors are naturally keen to get advice about where and what to buy and when. The problem is that the market is awash with spruikers, sellers' agents and mentors offering their services to investors. An easy way to measure the health of the housing market is by the number of seminars being promoted around the nation. In 2008 and 2009, when it appeared as if the Australian housing market would follow other property markets around the world and plunge in value, the spruikers disappeared. At the time of writing, they are back in force, promoting workshops and boot camps where, for a significant fee, they will reveal their secrets of success.

However, these people are primarily motivators and promoters, not qualified property market researchers, so how do they know what is going to happen in the housing market? The answer is that they rely on information and forecasts put together by data providers whose proven track records tell the promoters when it is the right time to start spruiking.

Promoters rely on the real experts because the information needed to make accurate measurements and forecasts about the housing market is extremely complex and costly to obtain and interpret. Consequently, this Holy Grail of information can seem difficult for private investors to access. Further, many investors make their investment decisions without even knowing that such information exists.

When I purchased my first house in 1973 I was one of these investors. Since then, I have bought and sold more properties, and been employed by two of Australia's major data providers, the Australian Bureau of Statistics (ABS) and Residex. My 30 years of investing in and researching residential property have shown me invaluable truths about the housing market, and in this book I pass them on to you, so that you can avoid the mistakes many investors make and get the best possible results from your property investments.

The motivation to buy my first house was purely to get my parents off my back. They were constantly telling my wife and I that we were wasting our money on rent. We had just married, though, and I had only recently finished my studies, so there were only two affordable purchase options. The first option was buying a new house in one of the developing outer suburbs of Melbourne, as all our friends were doing. The second option was purchasing an old terrace in the inner suburbs and renovating it.

Despite warnings from our friends and parents, we decided on option two and bought a dilapidated single-front cottage in

Hawthorn in 1973 for $20000, using $4000 we had saved as a deposit. During the next three years we spent another $6000 restoring the house to its former Victorian glory, and then sold it for $46000 — more than double what we had paid. Most of our friends' houses in the outer suburbs had hardly risen in value at all during that time, while our total investment of $10000 had grown to $30000, a tax-free capital gain of 300 per cent. This demonstrated to me the first truth of property investment — you can improve the value of your investment yourself.

Reinvesting the profit, we bought and renovated a much more expensive house in a sought-after Melbourne bayside suburb. Despite three years' work and a considerable amount of money spent on renovations, the house had only marginally increased in value when we sold it. I couldn't understand why one house had more than doubled in value, while the other had hardly moved at all, and no-one I asked could shed any light on it. Over the years I have learned that renovating does not in itself guarantee a return that is higher than the cost. It is crucial to correctly estimate the value that your renovations will add to a house.

That first house I purchased is now valued at $1 100 000 and it has provided its subsequent owners with an average annual capital growth of 12.5 per cent per annum, while the second house has increased in value at an annual rate of about 10 per cent. In fact, without undertaking renovations and by simply buying and holding, investors in Australian housing have received an average annual capital growth rate of more than 10 per cent since World War II.

I worked for the ABS in the 1990s on its first statistical publication about Australian housing. Published in 1992 and 1996, *Housing, Australia: A Statistical Overview* linked housing price growth to population change and differing tenure needs. This landmark publication provided a comprehensive history of the housing market from colonial times, and compared the various state and territory housing markets. It enabled me to understand why growth in housing appears to behave randomly, with many years of little to no growth followed by sudden surges that may last only one or two years. Further, I could see why this growth did not occur at the same time in each city, locality or street.

Once I knew why my second house had not increased in value over the three years after we bought it, I never made the same mistake again. Understanding the links between housing market performance, demographics and economics is the foundation of successful housing investment.

Some property investors buy in affordable suburbs with good rental returns and take advantage of the inevitable capital growth over time, while others seek quick results by renovating and trading. However, the housing market has much more to offer investors because it is predictable. During my time at the ABS I ran seminars that demonstrated the value of analysing trends to measure and predict market movements. In applying the rules of economics to the housing market I could see that it behaves like any other commodity, in accordance with the rule of supply and demand. Contrary to common belief there are no mysterious house price cycles endlessly turning to their own immutable laws; rather, there is a relationship between the number of people needing accommodation, the type and location of properties available, and the choice of renting or buying.

From these analyses I concluded that there is no secret to the housing market. It never behaves randomly or independently, it always performs in accordance with these principles. This applies to the housing market in a street, suburb, city or country. If it is possible to identify the factors causing market growth or decline, then it is equally possible to predict which areas will grow in value and which areas will stagnate or fall in value.

I was appointed head of research at Residex in 2005, where it was my aim to explain these essential dynamics of the housing market to investors to help them make the best possible investment decisions. Every movement of housing prices can be accurately predicted, as long as the underlying data is correct. When the housing market appears to behave erratically or under the influence of some hidden rule, it is because the underlying trends are not understood, or the information being used is inappropriate or incorrect.

This book was motivated by the thousands of discussions I have had with investors at seminars, trade shows and other property events during the global financial crisis and in the years following it. Many had made investment decisions that had turned out badly. Some investors had bought in areas that did not experience growth — or that fell in value — after their purchase, while others had bought at prices that turned out to be higher than market value. A few had sold at the wrong time and watched in dismay as properties rose in value shortly after the sale was concluded.

Some of these investors were the unfortunate victims of mentors and advisers who had given them poor advice or who had ulterior motives; most had simply not understood how the market that they were investing in actually operated. Yet, there were also many investors who understood the housing market and who were simply keen to share the secrets of their success with me.

My aim is to provide you with answers to the questions I am frequently asked. *Mastering the Australian Housing Market* synthesises my experience, observations and understanding of the housing market by taking you on a journey that examines how the market functions, and provides practical and proven methods you can take advantage of.

In chapter 1, I explain why the Australian housing market consistently outperforms other housing markets, providing investors with reliable and highly profitable returns. In contrast to the erratic and even disastrous performance of other assets in 2008 and 2009, you can be assured of the security of investing in housing. Chapter 2 shows you the unique benefits that Australian housing provides, explaining why you, as a housing investor, have a distinct edge. Chapter 3 gives you an insight into the tricks and traps used by those who want you to believe their claims about the housing market.

In chapter 4, you will learn how the Australia housing market works, with a brief look at its history. I explain how the great Australian dream of homeownership has played out over the years and why this works to the advantage of investors. Chapters 5 and 6 then get down to delivering results — how to achieve the outcomes you want, which housing markets will deliver them and where to find them.

Chapter 7 reveals the power of property market analysis and price prediction. You will learn how to use these cutting-edge techniques to make crucial decisions about where and what to buy and when to sell. In chapter 8, you will see how you can easily estimate the real worth of any property and use this information to ensure that you never buy a property for more than its value or sell an investment property for less than its worth. Chapter 9 starts you on your journey with an easy-to-use guide to preparing your personal property investment plan.

This book not only helps you to select areas in which to buy and to buy properties most suited to meeting your goals, it also shows you how to monitor and assess the performance of your investments at any time, so that you can make sure your goals are being met. As you proceed on your housing investment journey, I hope this book will become a frequently consulted friend.

Chapter 1

# Why the Australian housing market outperforms other housing markets

The Australian housing market emerged triumphantly from the global housing price crash in 2008 to 2009. Since then it continues to outperform almost all other housing markets around the world. Not only has the long-term growth of the Australian housing market averaged more than 10 per cent per annum, the market has performed with greater stability and resilience, avoiding the sudden surges and falls in value that have characterised so many other markets in recent years.

Growth in most property markets stopped and actually fell in value during the global financial crisis, with the exception of Australia, as shown in figure 1.1 (overleaf). In 2008, house prices in the UK plunged and the US housing market entered its second year of double-digit falls in value. According to the

US government–sponsored home loan mortgage corporation Freddie Mac, 44 US states suffered falls in housing prices during that time, precipitated by huge oversupplies and a general lack of demand. Australian housing, however, lost less than 2 per cent of its value in one quarter and quickly regained its growth momentum.

## Figure 1.1: Australia's housing performance compared with other countries

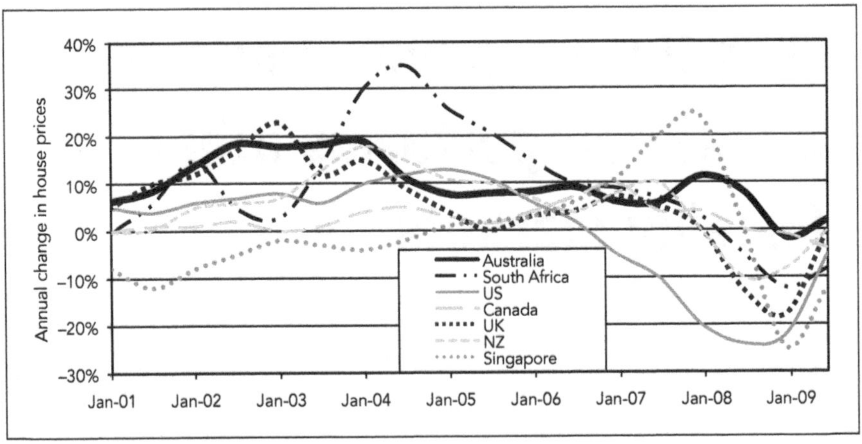

Source: Residex, ABSA Data (South Africa), Case-Shiller Index (USA), CMHC (Canada), Nationwide Index (United Kingdom), REINZ (New Zealand), URA (Singapore).

All of the major Australian capital city housing markets have continued to grow, with the exception of Perth. (The market in Perth suffered a downturn as a result of a temporary halt to the mineral resources boom, but it had been preceded by five years of double-digit growth, which left investors well ahead.) There are three reasons for the extraordinary performance by the Australian housing market:

➤   a strong and growing economy

➤   a high population growth rate

➤ an underlying shortage of housing.

Let's take a look at each of these reasons in more detail.

# A strong and growing economy

Having avoided recession, Australia's economy is now performing much better than any other Western nation. The reasons for this are our strongly regulated and robust banking system, which limited our exposure to the fallout from the US subprime mortgage crisis in 2007 and 2008, and the strength of our economy since then, which is rapidly aligning itself to emerging and growing Asian production markets rather than tiring Western consumption markets. China and increasingly India are becoming major producers and creditor nations and their own growing middle classes serve to provide new consumer markets. Australia is a major beneficiary of this growth through its export of primary produce and minerals.

---

**Food for thought**

Australia is larger in area than Western Europe and nearly the size of North America. It is a continent of climate contrasts, from tropical rainforests to deserts and snow-covered mountains, where almost anything can be commercially grown or farmed. This makes the country self-sufficient in the necessities of life and provides surplus for export. In addition, the enormous natural resources of minerals, timber, gas, coal and uranium are exported to world markets and provide a sound base for economic growth and stability.

Our biggest export markets for raw materials are as follows:

⇒ Japan—our exports include coal $25000 million, iron ore $8000 million, beef $2000 million and aluminium $1500 million

---

**Food for thought** *(cont'd)*

⇒  China—our exports include iron ore $24 000 million, coal $3000 million, wool $1400 million and copper ore $1200 million

⇒  South Korea—our exports include coal $5000 million, iron ore $2400 million, petrol $1900 million and aluminium $900 million

⇒  European Union—our exports include gold $75 000 million, coal $5500 million, and wine and beer $1200 million

⇒  US—our exports include beef $1300 million, wine and beer $800 million, petrol $750 million and manufactures $700 million.

Source: DFAT data compiled from ABS, IMF and various international sources.

Unemployment levels in Australia remain historically low at around 5 per cent and are trending down after a few shaky years following the global financial crisis (GFC) and the subsequent downturn in international trade and business confidence. Not only does the unemployment rate compare favourably with those of the UK and US, the rate is virtually the same in all the major capital cities. Australia does not have any economically depressed pockets or regions where unemployment leads to risks for housing investors.

Most of Australia's 22 million residents live in modern cities located on magnificent harbours, bays and rivers around the enormous coastline, each of which has its own economic focus. There is always demand for housing initiated by mining, manufacturing or tourism and where demand for housing wanes in one locality it booms somewhere else.

**Food for thought**

According to the Australian Bureau of Statistics, the major sources of economic growth in each state are different, as set out below:

⇒ Australian Capital Territory—public administration

⇒ New South Wales—business and property services

⇒ Northern Territory—defence and border security

⇒ Queensland—infrastructure development and tourism

⇒ South Australia—heavy manufacturing

⇒ Tasmania—processing of primary products

⇒ Victoria—finance and light manufacturing

⇒ Western Australia—mining.

# A high population growth rate

Australia is very young as nations go, just over 100 years old, and relies on overseas arrivals to provide new residents rather than on natural births. In fact, according to the Australian Bureau of Statistics, most Australians have at least one parent who was born overseas, and in the largest two cities — Sydney and Melbourne — most residents under 30 were born overseas. Not only has Australia accepted overseas arrivals more readily than many other nations, it actually depends on them. The continual intake of migrants is the secret to the nation's excellent economic record — it is how Australia has grown relatively quickly from a scattering of small colonies dependent on England for survival to one of the most envied countries in the world.

Australians are a resourceful and freedom-loving people who have fashioned an independent democracy peacefully. Migrant arrivals often come from war-torn countries, civil strife or persecution and they are determined to create a better future for their children. As a result, Australia has an unblemished record of resolving major issues at the ballot box and a national history of internal peace.

Australians have a positive and generous outlook, which is demonstrated by their historical acceptance of immigrants who are creating a cultural diversity and ethnic richness found nowhere else in the world.

---

**Food for thought**

According to the Australian Bureau of Statistics report *Australian Social Trends*, more than 50 per cent of Australia's residents have at least one parent who was born overseas. Following is a breakdown of where most migrants have come from:

⇒ In the years prior to World War II, most migrants came from England, Ireland and Scotland.

⇒ Between 1945 and 1970, there was an influx of migrants from Greece, Italy, Yugoslavia, Poland, Germany and Holland.

⇒ Between 1971 and 1990, most migrants came from Croatia, Serbia, Lebanon, India, Vietnam and Macedonia.

⇒ Between 1991 and 2010, the countries of origin were different again, with Sri Lanka, South Africa, China, Philippines and New Zealand providing the most migrants.

---

Throughout the period following the global financial crisis, the Australian Government maintained its policy of positive economic creativity and kept up a high overseas migration intake, in line with current thinking that immigrants create more jobs than they fill. The population grew by more than 450 000 people in 2009, maintaining its annual growth rate of 2 per cent, as figure 1.2 shows.

Figure 1.2: Australia's population growth rate compared with other countries

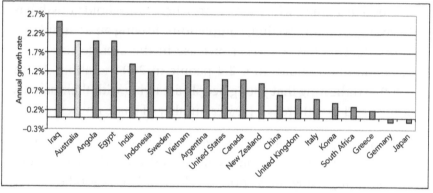

Source: *Australian Social Trends*, June 2010, Australian Bureau of Statistics; *Australian Demographic Statistics*, December 2009, Australian Bureau of Statistics; US Census Bureau; World Population Databank.

Not only is this rate of growth higher than any other Western country, it is almost double the world's annual growth rate. Overseas migration now contributes two-thirds of Australia's annual population growth; natural increase alone would leave us with a lower population growth rate than New Zealand, Canada or the United States. Even if housing construction was cut back, without overseas migration Australia would have a housing surplus and the housing market would be in similar difficulty to that of other Western nations.

# An underlying shortage of housing

Our high population growth rate has led commentators to agree that Australia is faced with a severe and worsening housing shortage. The Australian Housing Industry Association estimates that the current shortfall or unmet demand is more than 100 000 dwellings (houses and units, or apartments). Even the most optimistic calculations still reveal that a shortage exists. According to the Australian Bureau of Statistics (ABS), more than 160 000 new households are created each year. Housing statistics from the ABS also show an annual completion rate trending to 150 000 dwellings, with many years where household growth has been higher than dwelling completions, leaving an accumulated shortfall. This has led to an increase in the average size of an Australian household from 2.4 people in 2004 to about 2.7 in 2009 — indicating that young people are living with their parents longer and that there is a greater number of share houses.

The shortages are greatest where homes are in the greatest demand — that is, our capital cities — and these shortages result in constantly rising house prices and rents. This is good news for investors as it guarantees healthy returns.

## The opportunity for overseas investors

Most Australians consider the purchase of a house or unit an end in itself — just over one-third of all housing is owned outright by the occupiers while another third is being paid off by mortgagors. Of the 10 million dwellings, investors own less than one-third and most of this stock is held in the big capital cities such as Sydney, Melbourne, Brisbane and Perth. Yet these investors do very well, with rental returns averaging 4 per cent to 5 per cent per annum and capital growth averaging more than 10 per cent per year for the last 50 years.

In an effort to reduce the housing shortage the Australian Government has periodically introduced incentives for investors, such as negative gearing, which allows them to claim the cost of borrowed capital as an expense. The tax on capital gains is also set at half the rate for personal income tax. The government views investment in private housing favourably, as this helps to create demand for new housing.

More recently the government has gone much further, cutting the red tape for overseas investors and making it easier for them to invest in new Australian housing through the Foreign Investment Review Board. The government knows that encouraging investment in housing is not the whole solution — it must actively promote the construction of more housing or the housing shortage will get worse. Not only is the process now quicker and easier for overseas investors, but they are able to:

> buy vacant land for residential development

> redevelop existing dwellings if the development leads to an increase in the total number of dwellings

> purchase dwellings not previously sold

> purchase dwellings under construction or dwellings off the plan

> buy all the new dwellings in any development

> rent the dwellings privately or sell them without any restriction.

To many overseas investors, Australia may have only previously been considered a holiday destination — to visit the outback or Great Barrier Reef. All this has changed and Australia now offers overseas investors the best investment options currently available, with its housing market supported by government incentives, sound economic growth and low unemployment.

For Australian investors, competition for investment properties that is generated by overseas investors is good news, because overseas investors can only buy new stock. Rather than resulting in greater competition for existing homes, which is where Australian housing investors traditionally have conducted most of their investments, overseas investors help to increase the supply of new houses and units in the most sought-after areas.

**Food for thought**

The rejuvenation of worn-out inner-city areas littered with derelict wharves, empty warehouses and factory complexes generates a surge of investment and demand, which creates whole new suburbs. The vibrant new urban centres of Waterloo, Zetland, Broadway, Bowen Hills, Southbank and Docklands would not have been possible without overseas housing investment.

✦ ✦ ✦

Now is the right time to invest in Australian housing because your investment is based on security and profit. Not only does our residential property market outperform those of other countries, but you'll also receive far more important benefits to investing in residential property that give it an edge over other investments, as chapter 2 explains.

# Chapter 2

# How does housing compare with other investments?

Residential property is unlike other types of investments because it is a limited, yet renewable, resource. With less than one-third of housing being investor owned, you have an edge that other investments cannot provide. You can also improve the value of your investment yourself and there is an additional level of security, with the Australian Government actively underpinning investors' efforts.

Any investment you make is essentially a balance between risk and return. Return is the profit you make on an investment and the risk is that you may only make a low profit, no profit or even incur a loss. Bank savings, term deposits and bonds are considered low risk — not because their security is greater, but because the return is fixed, giving you a guaranteed return.

Gold, on the other hand, provides little return in times of economic growth, but can rise dramatically in value when economic conditions deteriorate. There is not a great deal you can do with these types of investments except to buy and sell at the right time.

Shares and property provide income from dividends and rents, respectively, and from capital growth depending on how successful you are not just in buying and selling at the right time, but also in choosing the types of shares and location of housing. As the complexity of each type of investment grows, so does the risk — and the potential return. Let's take a look at each of these investment options and see where they should fit into a balanced portfolio.

## Investing in savings and term deposits

Bank savings and term deposits are a secure and easy form of investment. Small amounts of money can be invested and added to at will and the funds can be readily accessed in times of need. Your investment portfolio should include sufficient amounts of savings to meet unanticipated property repairs or cover those times when other investments are not providing income such as property vacancies. It is never a good idea to have more than you need in cash or savings because money loses value over time — this is known as inflation.

There are times when economic pressures cause interest rates to become abnormally high, such as during the tail end of economic booms, or when inept or corrupt governments print money to cover their debt obligations. At such times, the rate of return may exceed that of other investments; however, your invested cash will still be falling in value because of the double whammy of high inflation and the income tax you have to pay on the interest you earn. Investing in savings and term deposits should only be used as a bandaid, to cover unexpected personal financial commitments and crises.

# Investing in gold

While cash is useful if personal disaster strikes, you will need much more help if there is an economic catastrophe. Fortunately, there is a commodity you can invest in that can see you through such times. Gold (and, to a lesser degree, collectables such as silver, jewellery and art) has traditionally been used a hedge against inflation and widespread falls in the value of shares and property. It is only because we have been spared the disasters that our forebears encountered, that few of us understand the importance of hedging our investments with gold. Gold can be easily bought and sold as bullion, and can be stored in vaults, bank safe deposit boxes or any secure location. The importance of using gold as a hedge is that it is valued precisely for this reason — its value rises when the economy or social system is in trouble and other assets are placed at risk.

When economic conditions deteriorate — for example, as happened during the GFC — the price of gold skyrockets. When the economy collapses, the stock market crashes, followed by company failures and increasing unemployment. The last time we experienced such a catastrophe was in the 1930s, during the Great Depression. The price of Australian houses fell while the price of gold soared, as shown in table 2.1 (overleaf).

## Table 2.1: house prices versus gold prices, 1930 and 1933

| Year | Average price of a house in Melbourne | Price of gold (per ounce) | Assessment |
|------|----------------------------------------|----------------------------|------------|
| 1930 | $4700 | $8.60 | Selling your house could buy you 546 ounces of gold |
| 1933 | $3800 | $24.15 | Selling your gold could buy you 3.5 houses |

Source: Residex and National Library of Australia archives.

As you can see, between 1930 and 1933 house prices in Melbourne fell by 19 per cent, while the price of gold rose by 180 per cent.

Although we all hope such events never occur again, there are indicators that point to when this is about to happen. The signs are soaring share prices resulting in an overheated sharemarket, speculation in commodities and land, inactive or corrupt governments and unexpected company failures. Governments slash expenditure while increasing revenue by selling assets and hiking tax rates. The main feature of a depression is a failure of governments to respond correctly to the signs or they simply give up altogether.

It is a far different scenario when governments, faced with inexplicable economic crises, attempt to tough it out and do so successfully, usually leading to a sustained period of hyper-inflation. This last occurred in Australia between 1972 and 1980, when we experienced basic commodity price hikes, record interest rates, union unrest, strikes and social unrest. While the price of housing soared, the price of gold went right off the chart, as shown in table 2.2.

Table 2.2: house prices versus gold prices, 1972 and 1980

| Year | Average price of a house in Sydney | Price of gold (per ounce) | Assessment |
|------|------|------|------|
| 1972 | $21 300 | $53.60 | Selling your house could buy you 397 ounces of gold |
| 1980 | $68 700 | $514.00 | Selling your gold could buy you three houses |

Source: Residex and National Library of Australia archives.

As you can see, between 1972 and 1980 house prices in Sydney rose by 222 per cent, while the price of gold rose by almost 1000 per cent!

In both the 1930s and 1970s, people sought the security of gold, the price of which soared in direct opposition to the economic circumstances. I am not suggesting that you sell your housing investments and convert your assets to gold — far from it — but I am reminding you that when conditions deteriorate rapidly its price starts to climb. It's easy to look at such periods with the benefit of hindsight and far harder to deal with them as they occur. No two economic crises are ever quite the same, because after each one occurs we build economic safeguards to ensure the same thing cannot happen again — but then something else equally unexpected does. As gold is essentially an investment of last resort, it is a good idea to have your own buried treasure, ready to access when conditions really deteriorate. When conditions improve, this is the time to extend your housing investments.

# Investing in shares

Many investors prefer shares when times are good and optimism abounds. They can be easily and inexpensively traded, and are an attractive first option for investors seeking dramatic capital growth that can be quickly converted to personal gain. There are some features of share investment — such as short selling, floats, franking, futures trading, margin lending, warrants and options — that can be confusing for less experienced investors, but the greatest trap of shares is their volatility.

---

**Food for thought**

Rarely would the value of a property fall to zero. It would take a natural disaster of huge proportions and even then insurance would cover most of the loss. Companies, on the other hand, can and do go bankrupt because of fraud, mismanagement or poor decision-making processes, leaving shareholders with the prospect of a substantial or even total loss of their capital.

---

Investors can sell shares quickly if prices start to fall, and this can and does cause share prices to crash — for example, as happened during the GFC. In contrast, it can take months to sell a house and it is precisely this reason that encourages investors to dig in and see it through when house prices dip. At the same time, share prices fluctuate dramatically as buyers and sellers compete for ever-diminishing returns until most cut their losses and swear never to enter the sharemarket again.

Between 2007 and 2010 the value of the S&P/ASX 200 (the most commonly used measure of share price performance) fell by about 30 per cent, while the value of Australian housing increased by 18 per cent. If it is unfair to make such a comparison when the GFC hit the sharemarket so savagely that it has yet to recover, figure 2.1 compares the capital growth performance of shares with property from Federation to 2010.

Figure 2.1: Australian share and house prices, 1901 to 2010

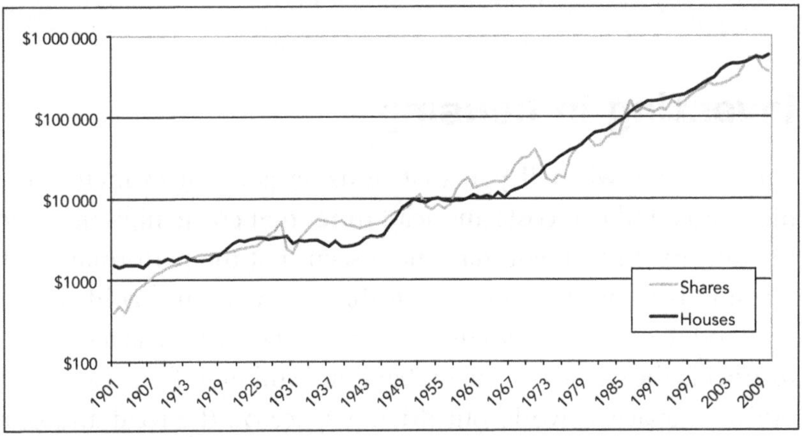

Source: housing data adapted from National Library of Australia archives and Residex; share index adapted from ASX published graphs.

The long-term annual capital growth rate of both property and shares is just over 10 per cent, but with the important difference that the sharemarket has taken investors on a roller-coaster ride full of thrills and spills. Australian housing only significantly fell in value during the Great Depression, and even then the fall from 1930 to 1937 was only 15 per cent, while the stock market lost 50 per cent of its value in the crash of 1929. Since the 1930s the housing market has suffered only a few temporary dips in value. In contrast, the value of Australian shares has fallen more than 14 times since 1901, usually in response to overseas crises such as wars, recessions and economic slowdowns.

Shares certainly have their place in an investment portfolio, but their role should be appropriate to the economic time. The oft-quoted maxim 'buy when prices are falling and sell when they are rising' wears a bit thin when you buy only to experience further price falls, which at the time of writing seems to be the case all too often. Investing in the sharemarket is perhaps best left to times not when prices are falling, but when they are about to stop falling, which occurs at the beginning of economic growth cycles, not when confidence is low and recovery from the GFC is still years away — in particular, in Europe and the US.

# Investing in housing

Some experts will tell you that housing is an investment with high entry and exit costs and lead times that create high risks for the unwary. In fact, you have now seen that the performance of housing is far more regular than that of shares and gold. There are good reasons for its security and regular growth. The territorial instinct is the strongest one we have and still manifests itself with our desk space at work, our driving space on the road and our housing. Cash has replaced bartering and shares are organised speculation, while gold is a symbol of status and sentiment. We need territory, on the other hand, to survive, to reproduce and to be safe.

Housing and land are essential yet limited resources, especially in our capital cities and even more so in the desirable parts of those cities. As towns and cities grow in size, the proportion of the most sought-after dwellings — those close to the city centre, or with a view or water frontage — decreases to the number of dwellings as a whole. Their value increases by comparison to the others as a result. Even in medium and high-density localities, there are limits to aspects and views. This means that demand for housing in Australia has always been a significant governor of price.

In contrast, the value of shareholders' investments can drop significantly when economic slowdowns and recessions occur. Not only are shareholders left lying awake at night wondering what has hit them, there is no compensation by way of higher dividends, which are the shareholder's equivalent of rent.

---

**Food for thought**

The mix of your investment portfolio should reflect the economic times. During economic downturns, cash reserves should be built up to cover possible increased personal financial need. Shares should be sold if necessary to protect your housing investments and your gold holdings increased as a final hedge against possible economic disaster. During economic growth spurts, buy shares and use their price growth to increase your capital as equity for further housing investments.

---

Although you cannot sell property quickly to obtain cash, in normal economic conditions you can borrow against property easily and banks are willing to lend using your residential property as security. If you try asking the bank for a loan based only on the value of your shares, you will find a very different story. In fact, the practice of margin lending led to many investors being financially ruined when the global downturn hit in early 2008. The bank will never attempt to take possession of your property, no matter what the housing market does, as long as you maintain the repayments.

While every type of investment has its place, the primary purpose of cash, shares and gold should be to preserve and grow your investment in housing, and over the next few pages I outline the unique benefits of housing.

## Everyone needs a place to live

We all need somewhere to live, and this underpins the security of housing as an investment. In short, everyone is in it. It is not a take-it-or-leave-it type of investment such as the sharemarket, where panic selling can cause prices to fall in days or even hours. Even when the market is slow, rents tend to rise to compensate investors for the lack of growth, and speculation is less common and usually easily recognised. In the case of a natural disaster, such as when Cyclone Tracy devastated Darwin in 1974, the government provided relief to the residents and both Darwin and its housing market quickly recovered. Compare this with the fallout after the dotcom bubble burst, when shareholders who lost money were left on their own and had no way to recover their losses.

However, while everyone is in it, they are not all in it to win it (or make money from it). According to Australian Bureau of Statistics housing and finance data:

> ➤ one in 20 Australian homes are government-owned public housing

> ➤ more than one-third of homes are being paid off by the occupiers

> ➤ more than one-third of homes are fully owned by their occupiers

> ➤ only one-quarter of all dwellings are owned by investors and privately rented.

In fact, more than two-thirds of dwellings are owner-occupied. The owners' motives are not capital gains or rental return, but living where they can afford, in a home with the right number of rooms and in a location that suits them. Owner-occupiers tend to buy with their heart, not with their head, and so may pay more than the market value. They spend an average of 10 years in each dwelling that they own and when they sell it is not to realise a profit, it is because their housing needs have changed. This can mean they end up selling for less than the market value. All of this gives investors a big advantage.

Imagine if investors purchased shares because they liked the suburb in which the company was located, or because the company was near a school or their place of employment. In such cases, informed investors would have a big advantage by buying for the right reasons — where growth is expected. It's the same with housing. Many buyers are unaware of the real value of the properties they buy and sell, and are not seeking to buy because good growth is expected. This gives you, the informed investor, a huge advantage, and means that you should always be able to obtain returns that are greater than the average returns in any area.

The same applies to renters, who move more often than owner-occupiers and derive no advantage from price rises in the areas they move to. They actually help to drive rents up as a consequence of their moving, because landlords are reluctant to increase rents if they have reliable tenants. When tenants leave, it enables the landlord to ask for higher rent from the new tenants. Owner-occupiers and renters are investors' best friends, because they create demand without actually participating in the housing investment market themselves.

## You can improve the value of your investment

Unlike investing in shares, anyone can improve the value of their property investment. For example, say you hold shares in Woolworths. If you go to your local Woolies supermarket and clean it up, decorating and painting, what impact would this have on the value of your shares? None. In contrast, you can easily improve the value of your housing investment by renovating, refurbishing and landscaping.

Some property investment experts promote 'property trading' or 'flipping', which involves buying a house at the lowest possible price, renovating it and then selling it within months. This is not a practice suited to everyone and it is not strictly investing in the market at all as there little to no reliance on capital growth. I provide an explanation of how to go about this profitably in chapter 6, but for now it is important to realise that most properties can be improved with a resultant lift in value.

There is another unique feature of housing. The government recognises the importance of housing to our national economic growth and supports private investors because they purchase and create demand for new housing. Tax and other incentives are provided to underpin the level of private investment. Not only can you claim deductions for improvements and maintenance, the Tax Office considers the cost of your loan (the interest) to be a claimable expense. In addition, the tax payable on capital gains made when you sell is set at 50 per cent of your personal tax rate. The government's logic is that by allowing investors to claim interest on rent or other income received, the rent that you charge tenants will be lower. The government subsidises investors to encourage the provision of more affordable rental accommodation, helping to reduce its obligation to provide social housing.

## High demand for rental properties

Unlike other investments, a return from your property investment is virtually guaranteed — as long as you buy in areas where there is high demand for the type of rental accommodation you own. In this regard Australia is unique, as demand for rental properties is higher than in many other countries. There are several reasons for this. Rental property demand is generated by very different socioeconomic groups, and this is why the type and location of your investments is so important if you desire a steady rental return.

### Positive gearing

Rental yield is the amount of rental income you receive in one year expressed as a percentage of the purchase price. If the yield is higher than the interest you are paying on the investment loan, the property is said to be 'positively geared' because the rent is paying off the loan for you.

While other investments provide income through dividends or interest, which rely on the performance of the company or the funds manager, housing investments rely on tenants to provide an ongoing return. Tenants will also usually look after the property they are living in, but in such cases where they neglect or damage the property there are legal frameworks to deal with and resolve the problem.

Australia has a steady intake of overseas arrivals who need immediate rental accommodation. Mostly couples or young families, migrants tend to prefer areas where they feel at home, areas where there is a large number of people from a similar ethnic background. In the larger capital cities, these tend to be older, middle-distance suburbs. Migrants are generally reliable and industrious, and their main motivation is to get established and buy their own dwelling as soon as possible.

There is also a pool of permanent renters, people who are on welfare or the age pension and from low socioeconomic areas. The government provides rental assistance to many of these people, and not only does this mean they have enough funds to live with some measure of financial comfort, it also means returns from rent in low socioeconomic areas that are actually higher than in more prestigious neighbourhoods. These areas tend to be former public housing estates on the fringes of our capital cities, but they can also be found as large unit developments in well-established areas.

The government continues to financially support low and moderate income households, the latest scheme being the National Rental Affordability Scheme, which provides substantial incentives to institutional investors who build developments for low-income earners. The benefit to private investors is that government-sponsored investments raise the ability of renters to pay and therefore push all rents up in those suburbs. This is typically how a government's well-meaning actions can have almost the opposite effect of that intended, by raising the demand as well as the supply.

In the more remote communities, government assistance plus the low price of housing allows investors to positively gear their investment. If you do not take out a loan to purchase the property, you can obtain a permanent and secure income from such properties.

---

**Food for thought**

In towns such as Bourke, Walgett and Coonamble in New South Wales and Wedderburn or Boort in Victoria you can buy a house for under $100000 and rent it out for nearly $200 per week. If you use all the rent to offset the purchase price, the house will have paid itself off within 10 years.

---

In addition, mining companies will often take out long-term leases on properties for their employees. In such cases, the rental subsidy can be nearly all of the rent. Mining towns such as Roxby Downs in South Australia and Moranbah in Queensland have incredibly high rental returns, with weekly rents approaching $1000.

Rental property demand also comes from the steady stream of new households created as young professionals leave home. Not only do these people often have good incomes, but they also want to live in areas that offer attractive lifestyles. These localities are usually the trendy inner-suburban areas of major capital cities, near beaches, bays, rivers or harbours, with access to recreational facilities such as gyms, cafes and entertainment. They seek new, well-appointed units and are prepared to pay the high rents that such dwellings command.

✦ ✦ ✦

Now that you have a good understanding of why Australian housing provides the unique benefits it does, chapter 3 shows you how to recognise and test for yourself the claims of those who will seek to sway you with emotive and 'insider' knowledge.

Chapter 3

# Who to listen to and who to ignore

Almost every day there is a story in the press or on the news about the property market. Our email inboxes are flooded with newsletters offering positively geared properties, never-to-be-repeated investment opportunities and gratuitous advice from experts who offer to take you on a journey to wealth from property. In this chapter, I show you how to recognise the doom-and-gloom merchants and boom-time spruikers. You will learn how to test their claims and save yourself the stress of worrying about a price crash that never comes, of investing in a hot spot that never gets warm, or of spending your hard-earned money on highly priced boot camps and courses that fail to deliver.

# The sky is falling! Don't believe everything you hear

When Chicken Little cried out that the sky was falling she quickly attracted a large following. The chickens saw the little piece of the sky that had hit her head and knew that doom was imminent. Foxy Loxy turned their panic to his own advantage by luring Chicken Little and the hens to the supposed safety of his cave, and they became his meal ticket for a month.

Predicting the future has always been a human obsession and, just like Chicken Little, we often get it wrong. Nostradamus, according to most readings, predicted that the world would end at the end of 1999. While we may be thankful that he was wrong, he certainly made fools of his latter-day adherents who claimed that his prediction was warning us about the millennium bug.

These examples illustrate that there are two very different types of event interpreters or prophets:

➤   analysts who get it wrong because they misread the signs, even though they have our best interests at heart

➤   spruikers who use our ignorance to their own advantage.

The problem for the rest of us is knowing who to believe.

Cynics will say that the easiest way is to wait, because eventually the prophecy either will come true or it won't. When it comes to the property market, we are surrounded by supposed experts who tell us how to invest, where to invest and when to sell. Housing investments are usually the biggest investment we ever make, and they can make or break us financially.

Some interpreters have hidden agendas, and try to lure us into potential property gold mines for their own financial gain. They invite us to take advantage of the secrets to success that they have acquired, when in reality they are selling highly priced mentoring and boot camp programs designed to feather their own nests.

There were many financial experts who misread the signs and got it wrong in 2008. 'House prices could fall by as much as 25 to 30 per cent in the next two or three years', 'It seems likely that house prices will follow the UK experience' and 'The price of Australian homes could fall by up to 40 per cent over the next few years', they prophesied.

People who took their advice and sold properties to beat the collapse quickly regretted that they had listened to these predictions. Waiting would have saved them unnecessary financial loss and trauma. However, waiting only works if the prophecy is false. It is the worst-possible option if the prophecy turns out to be right, and sometimes it is.

Luckily, there is an alternative solution — putting the prophecy to the test. Testing the prediction enables us to know whether to heed the cries of the doomsday prophets, jump at the promises being made by the boom spruikers, or ignore them all. I explain how to test these claims later in the chapter.

The widespread panic in the housing market that was alluded to in the previous examples was caused by the subprime mortgage crash in the United States and the ripple effect of the subsequent financial downturn in other Western countries. The analysts I have quoted used the crash as evidence that it was about to happen in Australia, particularly as our housing was considered to be unaffordable.

The most regularly quoted source of housing affordability is the Demographia International Housing Affordability Survey, which covers major city housing markets in Australia, Canada, New Zealand, the United Kingdom and the United States. The survey rates major cities according to affordability expressed as multiples of median household income to median house price, with 1 being the most affordable and 10 being the least affordable. As figure 3.1 shows, Australian cities are considered to be among the least affordable in the world with six cities or regions in the top 10. In fact, all of Australia's major capital cities are rated as severely unaffordable.

Figure 3.1: global housing affordability

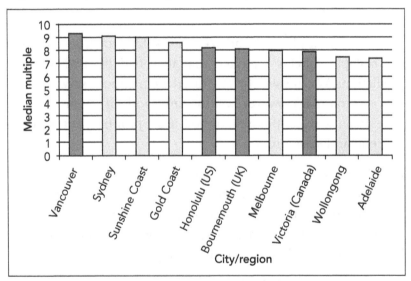

Source: 6th Annual Demographia International Housing Affordability Survey, March 2010.

Why did the Australian housing market survive the crisis years of 2008 and 2009 with growth, rather than the predicted decline in prices? And if we hear such warnings in future, should we take them seriously? For the answers, we need to look at the causes and effects of the subprime housing meltdown in the US.

## The US subprime mortgage crisis

In the late 1990s, the Clinton administration committed to the egalitarian aim of extending the benefits of homeownership to minorities who had previously been excluded. These groups included African Americans, Hispanics, low-income earners, the unemployed, the debt ridden and those with bad credit histories. The government was able to achieve its aim by relaxing lending rules and creating a new market for 'subprime' mortgages. The subprime market was made attractive to lenders by enabling them to balance the higher risks involved with higher interest rates. Unfortunately, many unscrupulous lenders took advantage of this, with disastrous results.

## The boom

A whole new breed of exciting loan options quickly became available to subprime borrowers. Interest only (IO) mortgages had an attractive low introductory or 'honeymoon' rate. Negative amortising mortgages (NegAms) allowed borrowers to pay less than the current interest only repayment with a higher loan balance and higher future payments down the track. Finally, adjustable rate mortgages (ARMs) would periodically raise or lower the interest rate as market conditions dictated. All of these loans were designed to mitigate the higher interest rate penalties being imposed on subprime borrowers and none posed any obvious risk, as long as house prices continued to rise.

In 2001, subprime and refinanced loans amounted to 15 per cent of all new residential mortgages. By 2004, these mortgages accounted for almost 37 per cent of new mortgages and, by 2006, they made up about 50 per cent. Even with higher interest rates, the subprime loans were attractive to borrowers as they assumed that continued house price inflation would enable them to refinance their way out of onerous loan terms, avoiding resets to higher monthly mortgage payments when their honeymoon rate period ended.

With the homeownership rate rocketing to record levels, the US economy (in particular, the building and financing sectors) soared. The number of new homes being built reached two million in 2005, compared with an annual average of 1.4 million during the 1990s. In the same year sales of both new and existing homes reached record levels and the volume of mortgage-backed securities collateralised by subprime mortgages increased from $18.5 billion in 1995 to $507.9 billion in 2005. These subprime mortgages and their derivatives were enthusiastically traded by well-established investment institutions in the US and abroad without any realisation that the assumptions on which their value was based were flawed.

## The crash

The problem was that, due to low fertility rates and the excessive building of dwellings, by 2007 the US housing market was in a state of chronic oversupply, particularly in the areas where subprime loans had been most enthusiastically embraced. Mortgagors suddenly found that their repayments increased dramatically when the honeymoon period ended. At the same time, rents for identical properties were rapidly falling, due to the oversupply of housing stock and the move of many people into the homeowner market. According to US Census Bureau figures, the rental vacancy rate in the US was nearly 10 per cent in 2007 (compared with 1 per cent in Australian capital cities). The attraction of ownership quickly dissipated when new owners discovered their repayments were beyond their capacity to pay, while renting was becoming an increasingly affordable option. Figure 3.2 shows both the dramatic rise in property prices that occurred until 2007 and the subsequent crash in prices.

Many new owners put their homes on the market to avoid interest rate resets or to return to much cheaper rental accommodation, but this only increased the glut of homes on the market and falls in value soon became widespread. House prices declined dramatically in many states between 2007 and 2008, with a national fall of 8.2 per cent. This left many borrowers with debts that exceeded the value of their homes, which meant they were unable to refinance on more favourable terms.

Figure 3.2: US average house prices, 2000 to 2010

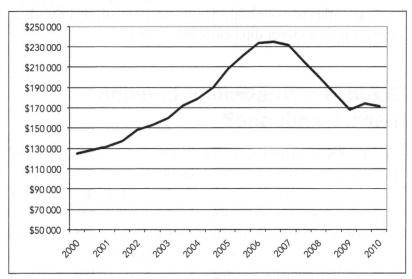

Source: adapted data from Freddie Mac, Fannie Mae and Nationwide.

Faced with the burden of crippling repayments, many owners walked away from their homes, giving lenders the option of accepting short sales as full settlement rather than attempting foreclosures, which would result in even lower sale prices for homes abandoned and sometimes trashed by their fleeing owners. By the end of 2007, the rate of subprime defaults was 13 per cent, rising to more than 17 per cent by the end of 2007, while subprime loans in foreclosure rose to almost 9 per cent. These short sales and foreclosures created further price falls, a greater oversupply of housing, and the virtual abandonment of new housing estates on the outskirts of cities such as Orlando, Atlanta, Miami, Sacramento, Los Angeles, Detroit and Minneapolis.

As the situation spiralled out of control it precipitated the financial crisis with which we are now all too familiar. While not as sensationally played out as in the US, similar falls in housing values occurred in the UK, New Zealand and most Western nations, and in many markets are continuing. The Australian housing market was one of the few to escape relatively unscathed, suffering only a minor dip before rising strongly.

## Could the Australian housing market collapse?

The forecasts of an impending house price crash are largely based on comparisons that have been made between the Australian housing market and markets in the US and UK. However, such comparisons are inherently flawed. The house price meltdowns that occurred in the US in 2007 and the UK in 2008 did not occur here because we have a rapidly growing population and an increasing housing shortage, while most Western countries have ageing populations, low fertility rates and growing housing surpluses.

We have already seen that Australia's population growth rate far exceeds that of other Western countries. Indeed, some have no growth at all or falling populations. Low population growth rates create less demand for housing and the housing needs of an ageing population change from standard family homes to medium-density units and high-density retirement-style accommodation. This trend has been accelerating in most Western nations in recent years as population growth rates decline. Not only are women having children later in life, they are also having fewer children.

At the same time, life expectancy is increasing, so the median age is rising in most Western countries.

In Australia the trend has been the opposite. We have experienced the largest annual intake of overseas migrants in our history in recent years, with the intake in 2009 resulting in two out of every three new households comprising overseas arrivals. These arrivals do more than just increase the population — generally, they are young, which keeps the median age lower than in other countries, and they need standard homes. This demand for housing is the cause of our relatively high house prices and the reason prices continue to increase.

This situation is completely different from the one the US and other Western countries faced before the subprime mortgage crisis occurred. Even the innovative and questionable practices that some lenders resorted to in order to obtain new business would not have precipitated the meltdown if the housing market had been in balance. Demand would have kept both prices and rents up, and enabled borrowers to refinance. It was the oversupply of housing itself that sealed the fate of subprime borrowers and their lenders.

In Australia, the notion that our housing prices are unaffordable and that current prices are unsustainable is not credible because they are a true reflection of demand being greater than supply. The future of our property market is, to a large degree, determined by this shortage, which causes a cycle of rent increases and price rises powered by the ability of households to pay. Sydney, for example, has the largest unmet demand for dwellings and therefore has the highest house and unit rents of all state capital cities. The growth in rents or prices in any area can be quite accurately measured by the number of new households, the supply of new dwellings and the ability of the new households to make rental payments or take out a mortgage. While this may not be good news for first-home buyers, it is an understandable consequence of the market conditions in our major capital cities.

No more than superficial comparisons can be made between the housing markets of Western Europe and the US and our own. This is why the prophets of doom and gloom were wrong and our housing market remains robust and continues to grow.

# How to test claims of a market downturn

When we hear predictions of a downturn in the property market, how can we tell whether to take them seriously? The answer is to test the claims being made using simple rules of logic. Ask yourself the following questions:

➤ On what basis are the claims being made?

➤ Is the research being quoted relevant and appropriate?

Any statement about the market should offer evidence regarding population and demographic change, housing shortages or surpluses and the impact of local economic conditions on them.

It is possible that the evidence provided is misguided and that the comparisons made with other markets are simply not appropriate. Remember, housing markets grow and slow at different times and rates according to local conditions. Simply comparing one market with another without taking these into account will result in inaccurate conclusions being made.

Always be wary of oversimplifications, as they are usually meaningless in the context of the realities of private investment. You are buying a single dwelling, or at best a few, so words of advice such as 'Sydney units are in a growth phase' are of no value to you. The housing market is very complex and no two suburbs, streets or even dwellings have the same value or respond in exactly the same way to changes in supply and demand. What is important to you as an investor is whether the types of dwellings in the areas you have selected are likely to perform in accordance with your goals. It may well be that their performance is not going to be identical with that of the market as a whole.

Even more misleading is evidence taken from one small sample — for example, unit sales in one area or over a short period of time used to support the entire market. You will encounter anecdotal evidence given as the basis for a purchasing decision, such as 'My friend's unit in St Kilda has doubled in value, so I'm buying there as well'. Some experts offer evidence based on tiny samples or none at all. Remember Chicken Little's piece of sky? This is a typical example of how mass hysteria or over enthusiasm can block out the truth.

Always look at the numbers being quoted, instead of the person who is quoting them. Quite often the facts do not actually make sense, but no-one takes the trouble to check because of the author's reputation. If there is no supporting evidence for the numbers, why trust the person quoting them?

Even if you are convinced by someone's air of authority and sincerity, it is still worth checking their track record. Thanks to the internet it is very easy to find out what any expert said a few years ago and compare this with what has happened. Consider the following when you are conducting your research:

➤ Who was right back in 2007 about the future of our housing markets compared with those overseas?

➤ Who predicted that interest rates would start to rise in 2008 and who was wrong?

➤ Who said that property in Darwin would keep rising in value in 2008 and 2009 when everyone else said the market had overheated?

> ➤ Who said that the market would not fall in value during 2009 when others claimed that the market was falling in value?

I urge you to check past statements made by experts — then you can compare their forecasts against the historical record. You can also check not just what they said, but why they said it — what was the evidence they used? You are welcome to use me as a test case and check my statements to see how well I scrub up.

Some of these experts will use and quote other authorities to back up their claims. If so, you should check what the quoted authority actually said and in what context this was made — it may have been in quite a different situation that is not appropriate to the property investment market. In short, don't take anyone's word for anything — always test their facts and credentials.

# How to test claims of fantastic returns

While the Chicken Littles may have our best interests at heart even when they make wildly inaccurate and unsupported claims about the housing market, there are other people out there who pretend to help us, but have their own hidden agendas to make a profit at our expense. It is harder to test the predictions made by these people because their whole purpose is to deceive us.

These 'experts' appeal to our traditional way of doing things, to our intelligence and to our fear of missing out. Their methods are designed to make us trust them, because once they have gained our trust, they are easily able to cloud the real issues. They will eagerly tell us about an exciting new development offering fantastic returns and offer as proof the fact that all the smart people or even some famous personalities are buying into this development. If that does not work, they will urge us on by insisting that if we are not quick, we will miss out altogether.

**Food for thought**

Just because an investment method hasn't failed in the past is no guarantee it will work in the future. Not only that, but there could be much better alternatives that have not been considered. Make sure you do your homework before embarking on your investment journey.

Always question any claim about the housing market that relies on emotion. Insist on all the facts and only the facts then test them yourself. Do they stand up to real scrutiny? As I urged you above, put their authority to the test. Ask yourself the following questions:

➤ Who are they?

➤ What is their public record?

➤ How accurate have their claims been in the past?

➤ Have they ever been investigated by the Australian Competition and Consumer Commission (ACCC)?

You may be surprised by what you find out. The more emotive their arguments are, the less likely that they will stand up under cold, hard examination. Do not be put off by their annoyance at your scrutiny of them. They may even tell you that your actions show you do not trust them, but the whole point is to know whether you can.

Investigation is the only way to separate the Chicken Littles and the Foxy Loxys who peddle emotive misinformation from those who provide logical and objective common-sense advice. It is essential to do your research because it is your investment that is at stake, not theirs.

# Build it and they will come

Some experts look for areas where housing has recently started to grow in value, and then use this information to predict that further growth is about to occur. They call these 'hot spots', hoping that the prediction will cause the growth. The increased demand caused by investors rushing to buy in such areas causes prices to shoot up further and voilá — the prediction creates the growth. As more and more investors pour in the prediction becomes a self-fulfilling prophecy.

The fallacy is that they are confusing the result with the cause, and investing in such areas is pure speculation. If enough investors come on board and buy properties, it can even cause a price bubble. When a bubble starts, the clever investors will have already pulled out, making their gains at the expense of the latecomers who stand to lose heavily when the bubble bursts, as all eventually must do.

House price growth will only be sustainable in any locality if there is ongoing demand that is greater than the supply. If the new households creating the demand are temporary, such as workers on a new dam or railway project, this will result in rental increases, which may lead to higher investor activity but only while the demand is maintained. Such hot spots can quickly turn cold.

If there is no housing shortage, then the demand caused by speculative purchasers can only lead to increased prices as long as the number of buyers keeps growing, just like pyramid selling and Ponzi schemes. As soon as the number of buyers slows down the bubble bursts. If there was little underlying cause for the price increases in the first place, prices can fall and collapse as panic sets in and investors desperately try to cut their losses. Although prices may eventually rise to their old levels, many investors will have been badly hurt.

## Ponzi schemes

Ponzi schemes are investment operations offering highly secure investments that provide very high returns. The profits paid to investors are mostly funded by money received from new investors. The scheme relies on more and more new investments to cover the increasing cost of paying profits. Eventually, when the amount needed to pay dividends exceeds the amount received from new investments, the kitty quickly dries up. The whole scheme then spectacularly crashes, with all investors losing their money.

The world's biggest Ponzi scheme was established in the United States by Bernie Madoff. The scheme, which came unstuck when new investors dried up during the global financial crisis, led to losses in the order of billions. In 2009 Madoff was sentenced to 150 years in prison.

There is no value in investing in areas where the only reason for doing so is that everyone else is doing it. Be especially wary if an agent or developer tries to convince you by claiming 'Be quick or you'll miss out' or 'These are selling faster than we can put them on the market'. These are not reasons to buy. At best, they may prompt you to ask for data supporting the actual demand, or do some research yourself to see whether the demand for investment housing is genuine and supported by a growing demand for rental accommodation in the area. While I am in no way disparaging the methods used by developers or agents, or their professionalism, it is only natural for salespeople to use whatever material they can find to support their claims.

# Watch out for scams

Investors in Australian housing have occasionally been victims of some elaborate property scams and lost heavily as a result. The gloss, glitz and promises of quick pathways to wealth were enough to convince these investors. In some cases, the developers teamed up with corrupt or inept local governments that control local land zoning and town planning to allow inappropriate developments to be made. In others, the developments were satisfactory but they were marketed in devious ways to unsuspecting buyers. Here are some of the scams you may come across — make sure you do not fall into the same trap as others have.

One of the most common scams is people being persuaded to buy land sight unseen. The salesperson tells you about the shopping centres, schools, proposed railway and magnificent new mansions about to be constructed, and shows you the proposed location on his plan of the new land release development. Every effort is made to induce you to buy without actually having a look at the development in person. The land is to be auctioned and prices are expected to be unbelievably cheap, or the deposit is so small that it would cost you more to inspect the land than what you are being asked to pay up-front. So you don't bother. How are you to know that there is no development, just rotting survey pegs in the bush showing where the boundaries are? Apart from a few tracks, there are no roads, services, water, sewerage system or power. You have to pay rates and loan instalments, and pay to keep the bush under control. In addition, the council informs you that you cannot erect a house unless the water, sewer and power are installed, which you will have to pay for yourself.

There are many locations like this around Australia — long-forgotten mining towns that have disappeared, past developments that died with just a few sales ever made or developments approved by suspect local councils. In each case, they have residential zoning, but these are blocks out in the bush. It is nearly impossible to sell them, with every other owner in the same boat, so after you stop paying rates and the council auctions the block to obtain the arrears you are left with nothing. This has happened to many first-time investors, particularly those approached by someone they trust, unaware of the real circumstances.

## The case of Russell Island

Some scams involve deliberate fraud, as was the case on Russell Island in Morton Bay, Queensland. In the 1970s, land on Russell Island was dirt cheap because the only way to get to and from Brisbane was by ferry. The state government made vague promises about building a bridge to the mainland, and developers bought up vast tracts of farmland and—because Russell Island did not fall under the jurisdiction of any local council—easily had it rezoned as residential. The inspection and subsequent mapping of the developments were hastily undertaken by air, resulting in around 20000 suburban plots being placed on the market. Investors raced to buy these seemingly bargain-priced blocks on an island that the salespeople assured them was about to become one of the most desirable outer suburbs of Brisbane.

It is 40 years on and the bridge to the mainland still has not been built, but most of the buyers' problems were more immediate. Many of the blocks were unsuitable for building on, with poor drainage and, in some cases, blocks periodically disappeared under water, as the aerial survey had been done at low tide. Most investors cut their losses and left their investment money with the mangroves. Although Russell Island now has many holiday and retirement homes and is a good investment location, the legacy of the scam still tarnishes the island's reputation.

Even when the development itself is satisfactory, there are several unsavoury techniques that have been used by real estate marketers to obtain prices that are way over the mark. The easiest is to sell the first few blocks in a development very cheaply, with sweetheart loans that encourage initial buyers to build quickly. Once these first homes have been built, it becomes easier for the salespeople to attract other buyers, for whom the prices quoted are much higher.

---

**Food for thought**

It is easy to get caught up in the excitement of an investment, but bear in mind that things may not be as they seem. I have heard many stories of investors who lost out big time as a result of one of these schemes. The tales are usually along these lines:

'They flew us to the Gold Coast for nothing. Not only did they put us up in a fine hotel, we had a free helicopter flight to view the new development. Naturally, we bought a block. They took two years to build the house and we couldn't get what we were promised for rent, because the area was way oversupplied, but how could we have known? After seven years of struggle to meet the repayments we had enough and sold out. We barely got our purchase money back because we had bought for double what the property was worth. It set our investment plans back years.'

---

These schemes can become quite elaborate, with potential buyers being given all sorts of no-obligation inducements such as free flights, accommodation, entertainment, dinners and a guided tour of the new development. The pressure is put on prospects in two ways — guilt and fear. Having enjoyed the free stuff, the potential buyers feel obligated to respond, and they are also continually being subjected to high-pressure sales tactics that ultimately induce them to sign rather than miss out on this never-to-be-repeated opportunity. For more scams to watch out for visit the Australian Securities & Investments Commission's consumer website FIDO <www.fido.gov.au>.

There is one rule to follow that will help you see through any of the scams or, indeed, any situation where you may pay far more than a property is worth. It is really quite simple: look for comparable sales of similar properties in the area. Remember, a property has no value until it has been sold. When you buy a new plot of land from a development or a new unit off the plan, the property has never actually been sold, only bought. It is only when you sell it on the market that you will find out its true value. In chapter 8, I explain how to do this. Find out how much other similar blocks of land have sold for and how much similar units in the same unit development have sold for. This information is the best guide to what you are likely to get when you sell, and that, after all, is what investment is all about.

✦ ✦ ✦

The next time you are offered insights into the housing market that promise to provide you with a fast route to wealth or warnings about an imminent collapse in the price of housing, you can judge which claims to take seriously and which to ignore. In the next chapter I take away what remains of the mystery and mystique relied on by the spruikers by taking you into the engine room of the residential property market, so you can see for yourself how it works.

Chapter 4

# How the Australian housing market works

The previous chapter exposed those who claim to have inside knowledge of the housing market or 'secrets' known by a select few. There are others who talk about house price cycles moving to immutable unseen laws that only they can explain to you. However, the truth is the housing market behaves according to the simplest law of economics — supply and demand. In this chapter, you will see how and why this interplay makes the housing market perform as it does and understand how to make this work to your benefit in selecting and managing your residential property portfolio.

# The great Australian dream

Australians have always dreamed of owning their own home, but housing tenure changes with the demographics of its residents and their ability to purchase rather than rent. The Australian Bureau of Statistics has identified seven generations of Australians and their housing preferences:

> ➤ The greatest generation are aged over 80 and live in retirement and nursing homes.

> ➤ The silent generation are aged between 65 and 80 and live in resort areas and retirement homes.

> ➤ Baby boomers are aged between 50 and 64, occupy empty nests and are investors.

> ➤ Tweeners are aged between 35 and 49 and are rebuyers and investors.

> ➤ Generation X are aged between 25 and 34 years and are first-home buyers and renovators.

> ➤ Generation Y are aged between 15 and 24 and are either still living at home or are renters.

There is another group that, while according to age its members fall into the groups just listed, should also be mentioned — overseas migrants. Let's take a look at these groups and their housing preferences.

## The greatest generation

Even before Australia became a nation in 1901, most of the population owned their own homes. The colonial gold rushes in Victoria and New South Wales had generated unprecedented population growth and decades of abundant prosperity. Large cities rose up from the old colonial capitals, with impressive central business districts, ports, railways and surrounding suburbs. By 1890, 90 per cent of households lived in homes that they owned or were paying off and there was widespread speculation in land buying along the railway corridors spreading out from the major cities. Bust followed boom in the 1890s, and the nation was born in a spirit of cautious optimism and economic stagnation.

The end of World War I in 1919 caused our first real house price boom, as returning soldiers and refugee immigration created a surge in demand for family housing; homeownership rose once again. This changed dramatically during the Great Depression, with new households finding that there was no finance available for them to buy a home. As unemployment rose to more than 20 per cent existing families unable to meet their repayments were evicted. By the end of the Depression only 40 per cent of Australian households were living in their own homes.

The generation born prior to 1930, known as the greatest generation, grew up in an economy with long-term unemployment and depressed living standards. As they formed new households and started families, renting was the only option available in an already overcrowded rental market. Rents climbed to more than 50 per cent of household income as the Depression continued.

They grew up during the Depression and survived the war, and were left with a consuming desire to avoid ever paying rent again, to hang onto a job at all costs and to pay off their homes as quickly as possible. Now aged in their 80s, these homeowners never considered using the equity in their family home to create wealth. To them, debt means only one thing — risk. All are now retired and live on the age and war pensions.

Their retirement plans have generally involved selling the family home and moving to a retirement village or nursing home. Although they created the postwar boom in housing, their impact on the housing market is only felt in the legacies they have left behind, such as instilling in their children, the baby boomers, the need to buy rather than rent.

## The silent generation

The silent generation grew up during World War II and the Cold War, in an atmosphere of fear and insecurity. They formed single-income families, where fathers held jobs for life but in many cases only had access to self-funded superannuation. They have benefited more than any other generation from the house price growth that has occurred since the 1960s by selling the family home on retirement in the 1980s and 1990s, and moving to areas that provide a more luxurious lifestyle such as the Gold Coast, Cairns and Cooktown in Queensland, creating huge demand for luxury apartments.

Misinterpreting this trend, some analysts predicted that growth in such areas would last indefinitely, not realising what the cause was. Developers responded to the prospect of continued demand with ambitious developments that have resulted in oversupply in these areas as the population growth rates slow down.

## Baby boomers and generation X

What does the future hold for markets with an oversupply of housing? While it is true that the baby boomers have mostly not yet retired, the real problem for housing markets in well-established coastal retirement areas is that when the boomers retire, they will choose different locations. Boomers created a fundamental gap by rejecting virtually all the value systems of their older siblings and parents. When they retire, they will seek pristine coastal or hinterland locations where they, like the silent generation, can enjoy the lifestyle that eluded them when the 1960s gave way to the realities of buying a house and starting a family.

**Food for thought**

Between 2008 and 2010, housing prices on Queensland's Gold Coast and in coastal Tasmanian towns (such as Penguin, Wynyard and Primrose Sands) have fallen, but for different reasons. Retirement to the Gold Coast is dropping as the silent generation moves to retirement and nursing homes, while baby boomers' retirement plans (to move to Tasmanian coastal towns) were disrupted by the GFC.

Once boomers recover from the superannuation and share-market losses they suffered, we will witness a grey tsunami of housing demand in coastal towns around Australia. While the Gold Coast will languish, Penguin, Primrose Sands and Wynyard will boom.

Of course, as this happens, an oversupply will occur in the areas they leave. These are in what were the outer suburban fringes and inner suburbs of the major capital cities 30 years ago, before they became trendy. In this situation there is no overall growth in population, rather a change in dwelling requirements brought about by changing lifestyles. The likely occupants of these areas in the future will be their children, generation X, who are starting families and buying their first homes in outer suburban areas. As baby boomers move out of well-established suburbs and head for their retirement destinations, these areas will become more affordable and enable generation X families to move in. This may well be an unexpected legacy of the boomers — their departure making such well-established suburbs once again affordable.

Another phenomenon the baby boomers have created is that they are the first generation to invest in property, willing to take risks and be confident of the outcome. Coming of age in an era of prosperity and self-reliance, they are not scared of debt and consider borrowing against the equity in their homes a means of securing wealth. Part of the roll-on effect of the housing boom most of Australia experienced in the early years of the current millennium was because large numbers of baby boomers began investing in housing for the first time, as their equity grew exponentially.

## Generation Y

The youngest generational group to enter the housing market is generation Y. These young people are forming new households and, for the next few years at least, will be locked out of the homeownership market. As a consequence, they seek to rent well-appointed modern apartments in areas within easy access to employment and facilities.

## Overseas migrants

The last group is overseas migrants. As mentioned earlier, migrants have two effects on the housing market. First, they create demand for rental accommodation (generally, more affordable units and houses in older suburban areas of our capital cities) in areas with employment opportunities and in suburbs where there is a large number of people from a similar ethnic background. Second, they are also keen to become homeowners, and the type and location of the homes they buy need to reflect the fact that they have been successful. Hence, the outward sprawl of our major capital cities continues, as well-appointed homes are purchased in new housing estates in outer suburbs.

✦ ✦ ✦

The movement of people from one type of dwelling and location to another as dictated by needs and circumstances continually changes the ratio of demand and supply in every suburb and town in Australia. While the demand for highly priced units on the Gold Coast is falling, demand for houses in other coastal resorts is likely to grow. High-rise units in inner-city locations such as Southbank and Docklands in Melbourne is only the tip of a demographic shift in demand led by generation Y. Equally, the outward suburban sprawls of Sydney, Melbourne and Brisbane will continue as more migrants seek to own their own homes.

You can see how differently each generation views housing as a direct result of their experience. Far from presenting a mystery to investors, this demographic shift in attitudes and values helps us to estimate the current and future movement of people quite accurately and, along with it, the types of housing they prefer.

## People create demand

The housing market is about people, their purchasing power and the places they occupy. Constant changes in this mix determine rents, prices and how they change over time. If you understand this relationship, you can build sound housing-investment strategies. Property prices have risen dramatically in the past when demand for housing suddenly leapt ahead of supply. In each case, demand was driven by sudden population growth, but the key is not just an increase in population, rather it is an increase in households looking for accommodation, and the type of demand is dictated by their ability to obtain finance.

At the end of World War I, Australia experienced its first boom in new households, caused by a combination of soldiers returning home and starting families and an influx of refugees from Europe. The same thing happened after World War II, with a much greater influx of overseas arrivals as the government embraced immigration as the answer to Australia's survival. 'Populate or perish' was the cry, and immigration provided the means.

Figure 4.1 shows how the postwar population increases — between 1918 and 1919 and between 1946 and 1953 — created the greatest surges in house prices Australia has ever experienced. Since then, the housing market has witnessed a continuing period of growth caused in part by years of hyperinflation in the late 1970s and 1980s. Up to this point, the Australian housing market had behaved in a similar fashion to those in other Western countries, but something happened that was unique to Australia. The rate of overseas migration continued to grow, and in recent years has overtaken the rate of natural increase.

Figure 4.1: Australian house prices and household growth, 1901 to 2010

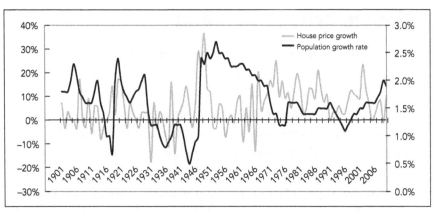

Source: housing data adapted from National Library of Australia archives and Residex. Population and housing data adapted from *Housing, Australia: A Statistical Overview*, 1991, 1996, Australian Bureau of Statistics.

The growth rate is now two overseas migrants for each natural birth, and this is the reason that growth in property prices has not really stopped since the 1970s. The rise in house prices has continued almost without pause, apart from one brief period during the early 1990s recession. This increase in new households can be measured and used to predict price rises in some areas and high increases in rents in others. It is crucial to understand that it is owner-occupiers and renters who create these booms and not investors, whose overheated activity in an area unsupported by underlying demand can only create bubbles, which usually burst. Nevertheless, it is investors who can gain if they understand what causes prices and rents to rise, and where and when this is going to happen.

To estimate the potential growth in any market, it is important to look at the population growth mix — that is, the combination of natural growth (births less deaths), overseas migration and interstate migration — and then overlay this with the changes in household composition trends that are occurring. Each new household will have different housing preferences in terms of where they want to live and what type of housing they desire, so you can then compare this with the availability of the type of housing that each group is seeking. This is not as difficult as it seems. Always remember that the housing market is about real people — singles, couples, families and retirees — who have real hopes and housing ambitions. When enough people have a shared ambition to live in the same area and in the same type of housing, this is where housing investment will be most profitable.

# Places create supply

There are about 10 million dwellings in Australia and only nine million households. This may lead you to think that a surplus of housing exists rather than a shortage. However, the reason this is not the case is that there are always a certain number of empty dwellings — they may be on the market, awaiting settlement, between rentals, undergoing renovation, abandoned, condemned or holiday homes only occupied once or twice a year.

In fact, the demographic make-up of our households has been changing because of the housing shortage. It has led to a growth in the size of the average family, as children stay home longer due to the high cost of renting. There is an increasing incidence of group or share households, particularly in inner-city areas, as the high rent can be shared and it suits their transient housing needs. Group households are also common in mining towns for much the same reasons.

The key to all this is overseas migration. Population growth caused by natural growth is to some extent accommodated by existing housing arrangements and only leads to increased housing demand when children eventually leave home or families expand to the point where a larger home is needed. Even then, there is an opposite effect caused by the empty-nesters seeking smaller dwellings and retirees moving into retirement villages. This is precisely the situation that is unfolding in Western Europe and the US, which is creating both a surplus of standard family homes in suburban areas and demand for smaller unit-style accommodation in well-serviced locations. Without the constant stream of arrivals, Australia would soon have an oversupply of units and houses in older suburban areas and in new housing estates in outer suburban areas.

Figure 4.2 shows the housing shortages in the capital cities of each state. Although it appears that South Australia and Tasmania have housing surpluses, this is not the reality. There has been a build up of unmet demand over several years in the capital cities, and in both states there is a large reliance on migration to drive up populations. This is because of the high numbers of young people who leave these states each year in search of employment or higher education in the eastern capital cities. Generally, they leave their parents' home when they depart, and so do not create more available housing, but the migrants who arrive need immediate accommodation. The rate of overseas migration to Adelaide now provides the city with a staggering 90 per cent of its annual population growth. In Tasmania the arrivals are mainly older mainlanders, but the net effect on housing demand is the same, providing steady demand.

Figure 4.2: housing demand and supply in 2009 by state

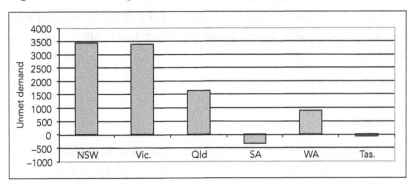

Source: Australian Demographic Statistics, Australian Bureau of Statistics; Dwelling Unit Commencements, Australian Bureau of Statistics.

The obvious question is if housing is so expensive and there is a shortage in our capital cities, why do the developers and builders not simply build more? The answer is largely because of our political system, which has two inherent flaws when it comes to housing. Virtually all emerging households, whether they are overseas arrivals or generation Y, want to live in the biggest capital cities, particularly Sydney and Melbourne for employment opportunities, entertainment, transport, education and so on.

We cannot control where people live or buy, so even though our urban areas are getting too crowded and densely populated, the demand for housing continues. As our cities expand outward and upward, the cost to governments of providing essential services periodically reaches critical points such as when existing water or power generation services are at capacity or public transport systems become overloaded.

This brings me to the second problem: our government has fragmented control of and responsibility for housing, which makes residential property ever more expensive. We have a three-tiered system of government — federal government, state governments and local government — each with only some powers over the demand and supply of housing. Each level of government is able to off-load some of the costs associated with urban housing development to the next level, while retaining most of the benefits.

---

**Food for thought**

The Australian Bureau of Statistics has identified the size of most capital cities compared with the rest of the state:

⇒ Sydney's population is 4.5 million people, which makes up 63 per cent of the population of New South Wales.

⇒ Melbourne's population is 4 million people, which makes up 73 per cent of the population of Victoria.

⇒ Brisbane has a population of 2 million people, which makes up 45 per cent of Queensland's population.

⇒ Perth has a population of 1.6 million people, which makes up 74 per cent of Western Australia's population.

⇒ Adelaide has the smallest population, with 1.2 million people, but it makes up 73 per cent of the population of South Australia.

These figures show that mainland Australia is a highly urbanised society. It is the continual growth of our capital cities that leads to housing shortages being far greater than in country areas.

---

The federal government is quite willing to encourage population growth through overseas migration, because migrants generate tax revenue and economic growth. Yet state governments have the task of providing new roads, recreation facilities, public transport, water, energy, schools, hospitals and emergency services. In turn, the state governments obtain revenue from new housing developments via stamp duty on property sales, which has become one of their main revenue sources. They also push part of the cost of providing roads and social, recreational and health facilities onto local governments, while overriding their restrictions on housing development. Local governments in turn place levies on developers to foot most of the infrastructure bill, rather than forcing existing residents to pay these costs. Developers in turn embed these levies into the price of housing.

**Food for thought**

Ever since Federation in 1901, Australians have preferred living in urban areas to the country. Australian social trends figures from the ABS show that while only 50 per cent of Australians lived in urban areas in 1901, that percentage grew to 60 per cent by 1920, 70 per cent by 1949 and 80 per cent by 1960. Although plateauing during the 1970s at 86 per cent, the influx of overseas arrivals is once again causing the number of urban dwellers to rise and this figure is expected to reach 90 per cent by 2051.

The federal government provides assisted overseas migration and population growth incentives, such as baby bonuses, because it gains the most and pays the least. Every other level of government gains little and pays the most, so their policy is to recoup as much of the costs associated with population increase onto the developers of new housing. This not only pushes up the cost of housing, especially in our capital cities, it causes lengthy delays in development approvals and discourages most builders from entering the residential development market. As long as our population growth remains healthy, this is not going to change.

# Purchasing power links people to places

In an ideal world, prices would rise by no more than inflation. The fact that this is quite obviously not the case is due to the supply of housing always being less than the demand. The urbanisation of our nation and the high cost of developing urban land has kept housing prices rising at a greater rate than the cost of living. Lenders control the availability of finance by setting deposit requirements, repayment rates, valuation rules and income tests, which determine when renters can move from renting to purchasing. When finance is limited, costly or simply unavailable to prospective first-home buyers, the demand for rental properties increases and the cost of renting goes up. Of course, the higher the rental costs, the greater the desire for homeownership, but there is another factor that can arise, and that is when the amount of finance that lenders are willing or able to put into housing finance is limited by external forces.

During the Great Depression, a whole generation of householders was unable to buy a home because the banks had no lending power — there was simply very little money available for home lending. Renters, on the other hand, were forced to pay rents that were so high they could not save for a deposit. Could this ever happen again? The answer is that it happens most of the time.

The shift from renting to ownership is determined by three factors: deposits, repayments and motivation. As a result, the instances when first-home buyers can enter the market in large numbers are very rare. Indeed, there have been only two periods in recent history when renters have made massive moves into the housing market. The first was in 2000 to 2001 when the federal government introduced and then increased the First Home Owner Grant (FHOG) — a popular incentive to first-home buyers that gave them most of their deposit. It coincided with historical low interest rates of about 6.5 per cent, and because the cost of meeting repayments was lower than the cost of renting, first-home buyers finally had the motivation and the means to enter the market.

An almost identical shift from renting to buying occurred in 2008 to 2009 when interest rates dropped to even lower rates than in 2000 to 2001. At the same time, the federal government once again radically increased the FHOG. The increase of first-home buyers into the market was sudden and dramatic, and pushed up prices in some suburbs by about 20 per cent within one year.

Lenders set up-front deposit requirements that are normally 10 per cent to 20 per cent of the purchase price. During times when finance is freely available and house prices are increasing, lenders are tempted to reduce this requirement. There have even been periods when some lenders have been willing to provide the full purchase price of a home. These are times when lending packages such as low-doc and no-doc loans have been offered to first-home buyers. The subprime crisis in the US is an example of how this policy can go terribly wrong if supply is greater than demand, resulting in widespread foreclosures.

## Limited supply means security for investors

One of the spectres that the supporters of share investment use to discourage property investment is that of affordability. They point out that housing is more unaffordable than it has ever been and is overdue for a huge fall, with the currently over-inflated price of housing setting investors up for a much greater risk than any other form of investment. However, this argument ignores one of the little understood fundamentals of housing and the reason for its much greater security — limited supply. The demand for housing is universal and fairly constant, so whenever property prices stagnate the cost of renting increases and investors continue to receive a good return. In contrast to the US and UK, rents in Australia continue to rise because we have still not dealt with the underlying cause of house price and rental increases — the housing shortage in most areas.

The constant demand for housing has meant that the only times when housing has fallen in value or the market has stagnated have been when finance was withdrawn, with a resulting increase in rents, as shown in figure 4.3. It is not generally realised that this is what occurred during the Great Depression. The price of housing fell by up to 15 per cent due to a reduction in demand that was caused by the inability to obtain finance, but rents rose dramatically at the same time.

Figure 4.3: Australian house prices and rents, 1901 to 2010

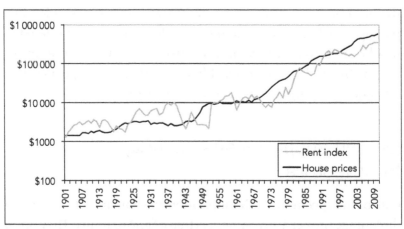

Source: housing data adapted from National Library of Australia archives and Residex published data; rent index calculated from assumed rental yields based on National Library of Australia archives.

None of us would want such a time of hardship and inequity to return, but it is important to understand that it took such a terrible event to precipitate a fall in house prices. Even then it led to a rental return that more than compensated investors.

The issue of affordability has risen many times since then, but in each case the reason that pressure on housing prices eased was a restriction on housing finance, not an easing of demand. During the 'credit squeeze' of the early 1960s, the federal government cut off the supply of finance through legislative powers it no longer has. In the late 1970s period of 'stagflation' and the late 1980s 'recession we had to have', record high interest rates stopped the flow of finance for housing. During the global financial crisis it was the inability of lenders to obtain finance and their reluctance to provide it in the cloud of uncertainty that prevailed. None of these crises created more than a temporary dip in the price of housing. During each period, however, rents rose as the supply of finance diminished, leaving investors with the same net result: an average long-term return of about 14 per cent per annum on their investments.

# What is housing affordability?

According to some experts, the overriding problem of our housing is affordability and a few continue to state that it is only a matter of time before the market crashes, as it did in the US and other Western countries during the GFC. Before this issue can be addressed, it is important to understand what affordability is. The often-quoted Demographia survey in chapter 3 defines affordability as the cost of buying a house expressed as a multiple of household income — in other words, how many years of average income it would take to pay off an average house. This is not a good measure, as no-one pays for a house this way, but it does provide a comparative value ranking between cities. As the survey ignores the actual cost of making repayments, which are controlled largely by interest rates, would it not be a better method to measure the cost of repayments on a median-priced house or unit as a proportion of average household income when a house is purchased?

The problem with this method is that it assumes every purchaser is a first-home buyer paying off 80 per cent or more of the purchase price plus interest in repayments. At the time of writing, about 33 per cent of home purchases are made without any finance required. These are usually people who own their home and are selling it to buy another one or empty-nesters who own their own home outright and are buying a similarly priced home or downsizing to a smaller one. The higher their current property is valued, the better.

Investors, who comprise more than 25 per cent of buyers, do not buy a property based purely on its price; they look to buy in areas that have good capital growth prospects, where demand for rent is high or where there is good potential for an increase in value from renovations. Further, investors offset the cost of repayments against the rent they receive plus their income, so measuring affordability purely against their income ignores the important rental return component.

Also, 33 per cent of buyers are existing mortgagors. These are current homeowners with some degree of equity in their homes who are moving to another house or unit. Affordability for these homeowners is their aspirational price gap — the price difference between the property that they currently own and the house that they desire to own. Affordability has nothing to do with the base price of their current property, much of which is probably now held as equity.

Less than 10 per cent are first-home buyers, for whom affordability can be measured by the cost of repayments as a proportion of household income. Even here, as you will see later in this chapter, the only option for potential first-home buyers is to rent or to buy. The real measure of affordability for first-home buyers is the cost of renting compared with the cost of repayments, not the cost of repayments per se.

---

**Food for thought**

Affordability is an expression of very different functions:

⇒ For first-home buyers, affordability is the comparison of deposits and repayments to rent paid.

⇒ For rebuyers, affordability is the price gap between current and aspirational homes.

⇒ For final buyers, affordability is profit from the price gap between home sale and purchase.

⇒ For investors, affordability is the comparison of repayments to income plus return from rent.

---

In more than 90 per cent of property purchases, affordability is not an issue. There is no doubt that Australian property prices are high when compared with other countries, and, as you have seen in this chapter, there are compelling reasons why prices are high and will continue to be so. However, the price alone does not make a house unaffordable for most potential buyers.

# The value of Australian housing is mostly equity

According to some analysts, the price of residential properties in Australia rose too quickly and by too much during the boom years from 2000 onwards and are overpriced. However, this oversimplification misses the point. The nature of tenure of Australian housing is ignored, as is the relative equity of most homeowners. While all of the focus seems to be on the entry of first-home buyers into the housing market, the fact that they enter at the most affordable point — a cheap unit, an older house or a house in the emerging outer suburbs — is not considered. They borrow the least amount that they can to be able to meet the repayments. Most people looking to buy property are not first-home buyers, and do so using their equity, not by increasing their debt.

As mentioned, more than one-third of Australian homes are owned outright by their occupiers, one-third is being purchased by their occupiers with some degree of debt and 25 per cent are privately rented and owned by investors. Looking at this another way, the total value of Australian housing is $4.4 trillion and the mortgaged component of this is $1.1 trillion. This means that three-quarters of the value of our housing market is equity and only one-quarter is debt. What happens when the market goes 'soft' — that is, when there isn't much demand? Vendors wait until selling conditions improve. At such times the only losers are vendors who have no choice but to sell — for example, deceased estates, divorce settlements or sales caused by work relocations.

The notion that property is unaffordable and that current prices are unsustainable is not credible when seen in this light. Housing prices in Australia are not out of kilter — they are a true reflection of demand being greater than supply, the variable restraints of finance and the growth in equity for further purchase that housing provides. These factors are what determine the future of property prices.

# First-home buyer markets

When individuals or households develop a need for security that outweighs the benefits of renting they start looking to buy a home. Some households, such as overseas migrants, will seek to become homeowners as soon as possible, because ownership demonstrates to them, their families and the community at large that they have been successful in establishing themselves in their new homeland. Trend setting — that is, when younger renting couples turn to homeownership, beginning a push among their friends, peers and a whole generation to do likewise — also plays a part. These sorts of trends can change the demographic make-up of certain suburbs and prompt developers to cater for it.

The problem is that the lender requires a deposit, which may be 20 per cent of the price, and this can be a significant barrier to purchasing. The lender may also insist that the repayments do not swallow up more than a certain percentage of household income, and this is where interest rates can be a barrier to purchasing for first-home buyers. The real barrier to homeownership for this market, however, is the difference between the cost of renting and cost of the repayments. It is only while it is much cheaper to rent than to buy that there is a degree of resistance to making a commitment to purchase. Using the high cost of housing repayments as a means of estimating potential housing price growth is flawed if it ignores the fact that the cost of repayments is measured against the cost of renting by potential homeowners.

If there is a period when interest rates are low and governments introduce incentives to increase demand, there will be a flood of first-home buyers into the housing market. These new buyers usually cannot afford to buy houses or units in established, well-serviced areas. They are forced either to new housing estates on the outskirts of the capital cities or to unit developments along city suburban growth corridors. This has an immediate effect on prices in those areas, because the incentives increase demand and generally do little to increase supply. When the First Home Owner Grant was doubled and then trebled in 2000 to 2001 and 2008 to 2009, the number of first-home buyers taking out housing finance soared to nearly 30 per cent of all housing loans. This was most prevalent in Sydney and Melbourne, where prospective first-home buyers had long found it almost impossible to raise deposits, afford repayments or obtain finance.

The result was an immediate lift in the value of houses in first-home buyer suburbs, which in most areas exceeded 20 per cent in one year. When the conditions that caused the surge in first-home buyer activity were withdrawn, loans to first-home buyers fell dramatically with the result that sales and prices in those suburbs slumped and even fell back, but still remained well above the pre-rush years.

## What does this mean for investors?

The implication for investors is clear. When the number of first-home buyers reaches huge proportions, this is no time to buy houses in first-home buyer suburbs as a few years of high growth is always followed by a price correction. The demand for rental properties in such suburbs (that is, suburbs with the lowest median values, which are generally located on the outskirts of cities) is always minimal to begin with and a sudden rise of buyers reduces rental demand even more, making both the rental yield lower and vacancy rates higher for investors. Renters, who are far more mobile than owners, tend to shun newly developed areas with a predominance of young, eager homeowners starting families because their demographics are different and they do not feel any sense of belonging in such communities.

## Food for thought

Melbourne's suburban sprawl is rapidly transforming former rural retreats on its outskirts into vibrant purpose-built outer suburban communities. For example, only a few years ago Mernda, 30 kilometres from Melbourne, was a sleepy country village best known for its local pie shop and football team. Mernda is now growing into a regional centre, with new housing estates and medium to high-density developments springing up to service an eventual population of over 50000. Mernda's population growth rate, at more than 18 per cent per annum, is the highest in Australia. Despite the apparent attractions, investors should avoid such areas until they are fully established and the first-home buyers start to upgrade, at which time good growth is likely.

Rising interest rates and worsening economic conditions can lead to price reductions as marginal borrowers bail out and sell up. In almost every situation, house prices are likely to stay flat for several years after the initial price rises until infrastructure and services have been developed and homes go on the market as some first-home buyers sell to move to more desirable locations. Most Australians will buy and sell several times before they buy a home for 'keeps' and it is these upgraders who set the growth wheels in motion. These starter suburbs have experienced little growth during their establishment phase, so they have a lot of catching up to do, and when it happens it does so quickly.

The rule for investors is to watch the new suburbs on the city outskirts as they become fully developed. This could be five years or so from the start of a first-home buyer boom, and is likely to be at the start of another first-home buyer boom. When interest rates have stabilised and the urge to buy has become strong enough with potential first-home buyers, any encouragement may precipitate another boom. It could be new or increased government incentives or rises in wages and salaries. This is the time to buy houses in such areas because they are now well established and will be the first choice for the more cashed-up first-home buyers when the next first-home buyer boom begins.

One effect of a rush of first-home buyers into the market that investors can make use of is the sideways ripple effect it causes. Once prices have risen in the most favoured first-home buyer suburbs, potential buyers constrained by borrowing limits that their lenders have imposed will start to buy in areas that are still affordable for them. This usually means they need to buy a house further out from the city centre, in regional areas or they may decide to buy a unit instead of a house. Figure 4.4 shows the price ripple caused as first-home buyer demand moved outwards in Sydney's western suburbs and regional areas in 2008 and 2009.

## Figure 4.4: the first-home buyer price ripple moves outwards

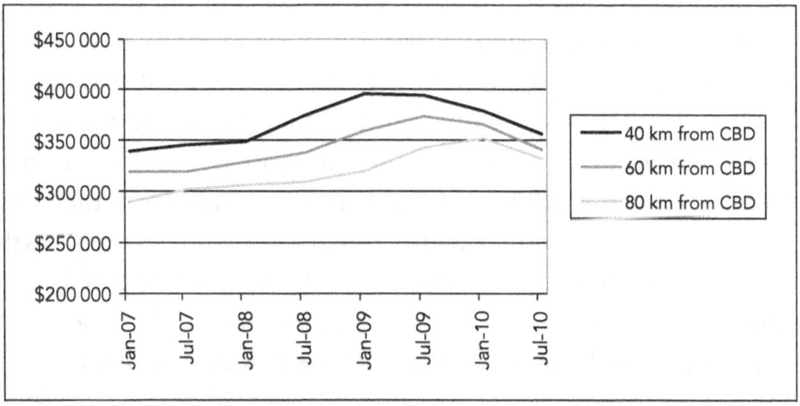

Source: adapted from published median house value and price data by Residex and RP Data for Sydney and regional suburbs.

This ripple effect will not occur until prices in the most sought-after starter suburbs begin to rise. Investors can buy properties in areas further away from the city or in regional areas with good services and access to the city. The price should be just below the affordability limit for the average first-home buyer. When prices in the better located first-home buyer suburbs rise beyond most first buyers' level of affordability, the sideways ripple takes effect and investors can quickly part with these investments after local price rises also push them out of the reach of most first buyers. Timing is everything with these sorts of investments, and properties are usually only held for a year or two. As first-home buyer markets tend to correct once demand has reduced, investors in such areas should watch the prevailing economic conditions closely. If finance is reduced, interest rates rise or government incentives are cut, growth in these areas will stop and they may even fall in value.

Units offer a different opportunity for investors as they can be located in areas of high rental demand. They are developed in sought-after locations such as city beaches, harbours, bays or rivers. In some localities, these developments are of sufficient quantity and quality to completely change the nature of a precinct and create new demand. They are sold to upwardly mobile younger households or investors and rented to generation Y. Units are also constructed in outer suburbs close to transport hubs and shopping centres. These units are sold to first-home buyers who cannot afford a house, and rented by investors to low-income earners and overseas migrants. Renting such units is relatively easy and you can obtain quite high rental yields.

The best time to buy in first-home buyer suburbs is when:

➤ rents rise steadily, making repayments comparatively less unaffordable

➤ there is a period of steady interest rates that restores first-home buyer confidence

➤ household incomes rise with no corresponding house price growth

➤ new government schemes lower entry costs or increase deposits

➤ lenders ease deposit levels and lending restrictions to first-home buyers.

Make sure you do not pay more than the correct price, that over-development is not possible and that you have picked the best area for future rental demand. Another side to a first-home buyer boom is that it is likely to reduce demand for rentals in precisely these units as renters leave and become buyers in first-home buyer suburbs. Reduction in demand will be only temporary and should not deter investors from unit purchase in high-demand areas.

# Subsequent or upgrading homebuyer markets

Australians will buy and sell several houses in their lifetime, moving on average every seven to 10 years. The reasons for this are because the family is growing, their income has increased and they want to be seen as more successful, they want to live closer to their work or be nearer to family. As first-home buyers usually cannot afford to buy where they would prefer to live, it takes several moves before they are financially able to buy in their perfect location, and, of course, the perfect location itself changes with their lifestyle and aspirations.

These upgraders comprise all those households who have made the transition to homeownership, but are still paying off their mortgage. They represent around one-third of all Australian households. While in their first home, they are at the mercy of interest rate and income fluctuations that can cause considerable stress if they become too difficult to manage. Over time, however, this exposure to risk diminishes and their financial position becomes more comfortable.

As both repayments and capital growth are constantly increasing the equity they have in their home, they are no longer like first-home buyers. This is because the comparative cost of renting is no longer an issue, they have equity instead of a deposit, they have a proven repayment record and their loan repayments are gradually reducing as a percentage of household income. For this group of homeowners, affordability now becomes a measure of the equity in their home compared with the price of a new home and their ability to meet the new loan repayments. It means that each move is usually upward to a more desirable home or a more sought-after location that they can now afford.

This continual turnover of properties presents excellent opportunities for investors, because owner-occupiers buy and sell properties for personal reasons. It may be a buyer's market rather than a good time to sell, but many homeowners would not be aware of this. The area they move to may be a seller's market, with few listed properties and, again, they may be unaware of the nature of the property market in the area. This is why investors who research these facts will always achieve more than the long-term growth rate in any area, because they are buying and selling at the right time to make the maximum gain.

As figure 4.5 (overleaf) shows, the significant entry of first-home buyers into the Sydney market in 2008 and 2009 caused a price ripple through the housing market as each group of homeowners took their increased equity and moved to a new dwelling or area. An excessively high growth rate will cause a correction if the conditions that resulted in the entry of first-home buyers are changed and this correction also flows up through the market, as figure 4.5 shows. If, however, the conditions that encourage first-home buyers into the market are not adversely changed, then the growth will continue as long as first-home buyers continue to enter the market in large numbers.

## Figure 4.5: the first-home buyer price ripple moves upwards

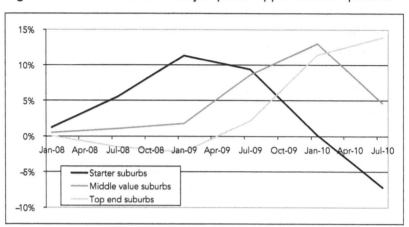

Source: adapted from published median house value and price data by Residex and RP Data for Sydney suburbs.

Fortunately for investors, it is possible to predict where and when such price rises will occur. The best time to buy in upgrader markets is when:

➤ there is a long period of little to no growth in the first-home buyer market

➤ first-home buyers are entering the market in greater numbers

➤ economic conditions are good and unemployment levels are low

➤ finance is freely available to existing homeowners.

It is easy to estimate where the sellers and buyers moving up the desirability ladder will move to simply by knowing the median value of suburbs. This is how many spruikers give the impression of having some sort of inside knowledge, when all they are doing is reading the direction that the market is moving.

# Final homebuyer markets

Final homebuyers are baby boomers whose children have long since left the family home. Having progressively moved through the various stages of homeownership, they usually have full equity in a home that has risen in value many times since they bought it. These homes are also generally well above the median value for the city or town they live in, or they have used this equity to make substantial investments.

The influence this group has on house prices is directly proportional to the value of stock they own as the percentage of the total. In localities and cities where population growth is slow and ageing, the steadying effect that they put on prices is far greater than in high population growth cities where interest rate changes can significantly affect house prices. Baby boomers hold their homes far longer than first or second homebuyers, which has a dampening effect on property prices. Cynics may argue that the only time this group ever makes a positive impact on the housing market is when they pass away and leave the home to their children to sell and use the legacy for a deposit on their own first homes.

However, nothing could be further from the truth. This group of homeowners presents enormous benefits to investors, many of who are also baby boomers. They own about one-third of Australian property as homes, holiday homes and investments, generally without any mortgage, and when they decide to retire it will be to locations that are attractive and practical for their retirement. Their final homes are likely to cost less than the ones they own, so their equity will not only cover the cost, but will usually leave them with something left over. For these homeowners, the purchase of a last home has nothing to do with affordability. It is purely a matter of deciding on the best area that meets their needs.

The buying power they exercise is enormous, and as they move to retirement locations the equity they have provides them with the ability to purchase whatever and wherever they want. Since the global financial crisis, which knocked the stuffing out of their superannuation and sharemarket investments, most of the boomers have put off retirement until they recoup some of their lost investments.

When they do retire, boomers will not be moving to the most popular retirement areas of the last 20 years such as the Gold Coast, Nelson Bay, Byron Bay or Hervey Bay. The reason is that these are the retirement locations chosen by their older siblings and parents, and there is a bigger generation gap between baby boomers and the ones before than with any other generation. Generally, they have a much closer bond with their generation X children than their parents or older siblings had with them. Unlike previous generations, whose dream was to move north and retire in luxury near the beach, boomers will want to stay near their children and grandchildren. They will retire to coastal and rural areas a couple of hours' drive away from their grandchildren.

Baby boomers will start to leave the workforce en masse when their superannuation and sharemarket holdings are back to the levels they were in 2007, before the crash. As their friends and colleagues leave the workforce, they will have less motivation to stay on in rapidly changing work environments. Some may simply be forced out as changing practices and technology make them redundant. The best time to invest in final homebuyer markets is:

➤ before the sharemarket reaches its pre-GFC levels (when the S&P/ASX 200 rises to more than 6500 points)

➤ when superannuation funds are recovering the losses they made in 2008 and 2009

> ➤ when there is plenty of anecdotal evidence that baby boomers are retiring

> ➤ the sooner the better and certainly within the next few years.

They will have an enormous impact on property prices when they move, because there are around two million baby boomer households in Australia, which is equivalent to the entire number of households in Sydney, our largest city. They will want to move to smaller, undeveloped locations and the pressure on prices in those areas will be enormous. Plus, they will have the cash to pay whatever is the asking price.

The crucial question is where will they move? You can narrow the search of likely retirement areas down to coastal and riverside or rural retreats that are within one or two hours by car or plane from capital cities. These areas include:

> ➤ the less developed areas of the Central Coast and Hunter Valley in New South Wales

> ➤ the Mornington and Bellarine Peninsulas in Victoria, and the coastal strips along the eastern and southern coastlines

> ➤ coastal resorts, such as the Whitsundays in Queensland, and the Fleurieu and Yorke Peninsula coastal towns in South Australia.

Tasmania or the south coast of New South Wales may seem too far away for many retirees, but figure 4.6 (overleaf) shows some unspoiled havens. They are on Tasmania's northern coastline, near Hobart and on the South Coast of New South Wales, and are accessible by car and plane within 90 minutes of Melbourne or Sydney. A boom in such coastal towns near major airports is imminent.

## Figure 4.6: Price growth in areas 90 minutes from Sydney or Melbourne

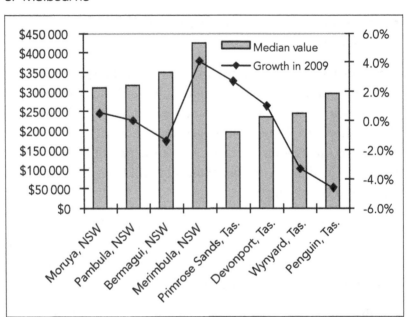

Source: adapted from published median house value and price data by Residex.

Of course, not all baby boomers will move, and some will opt for high-rise luxury living in inner-city and premium suburban locations. Others will buy holiday homes in retirement areas and make a gradual shift to retirement. Even so, the sheer weight of their numbers and buying power will cause a fundamental paradigm shift in housing values, such as we have never witnessed. There is of course, a flip side to this massive relocation: for every purchase there is a sale, and the impact on well-established higher end suburbs in capital cities will be noticeable as baby boomers move out. It will not be as dramatic as the movement in prices where they move to, because the housing supply and demand mix in those older suburbs is dependent on many other factors, but it could lead to reductions in prices in some suburbs.

✦ ✦ ✦

Having explored how the housing market works in Australia, you will also have seen how each of the buyer and seller markets can work to your benefit as an investor. The difference between owner-occupiers and investors should also now be clear — that there may be many forces that motivate owner-occupiers and many compromises that they have to make, while the motivation for investors is always to achieve growth and return. Chapter 5 shows you when to invest to get the results you want.

# Chapter 5

# How to get the results you want

When you buy a home to live in there are many emotional and financial considerations that usually lead to a trade-off between the type of home you want to live in, where it is located and how much you can afford to pay. When you buy an investment property, however, there should be no emotional considerations. The type of dwelling, its condition and location must be determined by the outcomes you are expecting to obtain from the investment.

In this chapter I look at the various investment outcomes you can achieve from property:

➤ high capital growth in a short period of time

➤ investments that pay for themselves

➤ consistently high growth with low risk.

I will then weigh up the benefits of buying in the city or the country, and examine what effect climate change has had on the property market. Throughout the chapter I will show you where and what to invest in.

## High capital growth in a short period of time

So, you're hungry for high capital growth in a short period of time? You will need to know where the highest capital growth areas are in Australia and what drives the housing prices in those areas relentlessly upwards. Investors who want high returns are usually prepared to take some risks, but I will show you areas of extraordinary high growth that are virtually risk free, and how to anticipate any possible risks.

For most of Australia's history, we have lived on the wealth of the land. At first it was fine Merino wool and later wheat paid the cost of developing cities and ports along our coastlines, major rivers and railway towns. These became boom towns when economic conditions were good and ghost towns when depressions and recessions hit. Our economy was so firmly linked to Britain's, that when the British Government cut finance to the Australian colonies in 1890, the economy collapsed and we entered the worst depression we have ever had. The stock market lost 80 per cent of its value and the housing market plunged by 50 per cent, not recovering its value for nearly 30 years.

There were three reasons for this — widespread speculation in land, housing and commodities reached epidemic proportions, unregulated financial and trading systems and dependence on

Great Britain for finance. Rather than relying on revenue from export commodities, the Australian colonies used British capital as an ongoing source of wealth. It was beyond the capacity of the tiny colonial economies to remain sustainable without further borrowing, and when the British banks cut the flow of funds the colonial economies collapsed.

During the years of economic expansion, ports and railway towns experienced the most spectacular growth, many of which are now shadows of their former selves, no longer relevant in the age of road transport. Similarly, we have experienced mining booms, and the Australian countryside is littered with dead or decaying mining towns that once enjoyed immense wealth and fame. Tasmania, for example, had mines such as Mount Bischof and Mount Lyell, which at the turn of the 20th century were the biggest tin and copper mines in the world. Mines such as these created and supported populations in their thousands. Today, the only real gains that these and other places such as Waratah, Queenstown, Beaconsfield and Zeehan in Tasmania get is from tourism.

It is the same all over Australia — mining towns tend to boom and bust, sometimes several times during their history, according to the demand for what the mines produce and their capacity to produce it. Some mining towns have extremely long lives, such as Mount Isa in Queensland and Broken Hill in New South Wales, and still maintain a high rate of production, but the housing market in those towns behaves no differently from any other city.

## Mining towns can have high capital growth rates

The highest short-term capital growth rates and highest rental returns are found in mining towns. These towns have several unique features, one of which is the demographic of their main inhabitants. Miners usually work on contracts and will leave when the contract ends. Most will seek rental accommodation and, in many cases, the mining company leases houses and units from investors and then provides them to their employees at huge subsidies. For those investors lucky enough to obtain such a lease, rental returns of more than 10 per cent are not uncommon. The high rental yields create investor interest and this in turn leads to price increases. In booming mining towns, periods of high rental yield are invariably followed by years of high capital growth, and in some towns both are experienced at the same time.

The best long-term performing town in Australia is Moranbah, a mining town in Queensland's Surat Basin where black coal is being mined on an enormous scale. According to Residex, Moranbah's annual average capital growth rate between 2000 and 2010 is more than 22 per cent per annum and the total average annual return (including rent) is more than 31 per cent. According to RP Data, Moranbah's capital growth between 2005 and 2010 totalled nearly 90 per cent. Yet, there were investors who considered selling out during the global financial crisis because the mining companies cut employment numbers as the price of thermal coal dropped. Then the investors discovered that although the price had dropped, the demand remained the same.

What makes thermal coal special is that its demand is fairly constant, even if the price fluctuates, because it is used to generate electricity. The major importers of our thermal coal are Japan, buying $24 billion worth each year, followed by Europe and South Korea. Even though these countries have not recovered from the GFC and their economies are shaky, they still need thermal coal. As a result of this ongoing demand, thermal coalmining towns form the best investment areas for short-term growth in Australia.

## The stages of a mining town

Unfortunately, achieving high capital growth is not quite as easy as simply buying in a mining town. These towns go through various stages and it is crucial to invest at the right time. As figure 5.1 shows, there are six stages to a mine's life: discovery, development, production, expansion, further expansion, decline and closure. Property price growth is related to the number of people coming into the town to live or departing.

Figure 5.1: the six stages of a mining town

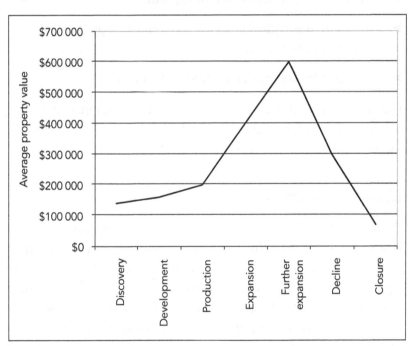

During the discovery and development stages, there may be slow growth in prices, but nothing compared with when the mine starts production. It is at this point that the town reaches its highest population to date, and if there is no expansion, that's as far as prices will go. Most mines undergo one or more expansion phases and sometimes partial closures, but these further expansion phases are when the really spectacular house price growth occurs, because the housing market is fully stretched and the mining company is operating a successful venture and is desperate to employ more labour. This is when the companies start offering investors long-term leases on very high rental yields and this encourages more investors to join the bandwagon.

The best time to invest in mining towns and their ports is when:

➤ there is no other accommodation than in the mining town

➤ the mine is about to open or expand

➤ the mine has sufficient easily recoverable high-grade deposits to last for years

➤ demand for the mineral being mined is rising.

It should be noted that there are several different types of mining towns and each have different conditions, and it is important to understand what these conditions are.

## Coalmining towns

Coalmining towns, especially those mining thermal coals, are relatively immune to the economic conditions in the importing countries; however, they are always in danger of running out of coal or of the quality of coal reducing. This causes the mining company to cut back production, or close the mine and open another in a more suitable location. Despite the enormous reserves of high-grade coal in Queensland's Surat and Bowen basins, coalmines are continually being closed down and new ones developed. If you are looking to invest in a Queensland coalmining town, you should undertake careful due diligence to ascertain the expected life of mines in the town's vicinity, and whether other mines are proposed in the area.

Just as important to coalmining as the dormitory towns they support are the ports from where the coal is loaded and shipped overseas. Huge ports in Queensland such as Hay Point and Abbot Point are excellent investment areas when coal demand is rising and the ports need expansion and maintenance, bringing in hundreds of extra residents.

Some of the Queensland coalmining towns and ports operating at the time of writing include:

➤ Wandoan — the site of a recently announced mining project

➤ Bowen — near the huge Abbot Point coal loading terminal

➤ Moranbah — growth continues and rental returns are more than 7 per cent

➤ Collinsville — an older coalmining town about to undergo expansion

➤ Hay Point — a coal-loading terminal about to be expanded.

Another area of Australia that is rich in black coal is the Hunter Region, inland from Newcastle in New South Wales. Here, long-established mining towns provide accommodation for generations of coalminers and the stability of demand makes them less appealing to investors. The coal-loading port of Newcastle is also a major city (it is bigger than some capital cities) and its welfare does not depend on the coal-export market. This could change with the development of the enormously rich Gunnedah Basin coal deposits. This development is being opposed by local farmers as the area holds some of the most productive farmland in Australia. When announcements of the proposed development were made in 2008, investors moved into nearby towns such as Gunnedah, Curlewis, Werris Creek and Quirindi, buying up residential stock.

It will take years for these mines to be developed, and even longer for production to start, as the project is still in the feasibility stage. As seen in figure 5.1, real price growth does not occur until the development and production stages, so most of the investors have long waits ahead of them and, judging by recent price falls in those towns, some have got cold feet already.

## Iron ore mines

If coal is the mineral of the east, then iron ore is the mineral of the west. The world's biggest iron ore mine is located at Mount Newman in Western Australia. The iron ore was discovered in the 1990s, but it was too far away from the industrialised economies that might need it. Development proceeded slowly until the Chinese Government started a policy of rapid industrialisation. It needed all the iron ore it could buy, and Mount Newman had the richest deposit and was close to China.

It quickly became clear that China would take all the iron ore possible, and the mine expanded rapidly. The ore went to Port Hedland, a sleepy fishing village where a house worth $40 000 when iron ore was discovered in 1992 was worth $200 000 in 2002 when mine development started. It rose again to $400 000 when the mine was expanded in 2005. Five years and several mine expansions later, the median price of a house in Port Hedland is $1.1 million.

Port Hedland has Australia's second-highest average growth rate over 10 years at 18 per cent per year, behind Moranbah. Some investors sold out in 2005 at $400 000, believing house prices had peaked. They missed the golden rule of housing investment: if the conditions for growth remain, then the growth will continue. Mining towns are unlike suburban areas, where if the price rises in one suburb, buyers can look somewhere else. In Port Hedland there are no other options and the mine keeps expanding, so prices keep going up.

## Other types of mines

This situation — that is, workers having nowhere else to live — is common in many mining towns that are in remote places and rely on dormitory towns, such as Roxby Downs in South Australia, that have been especially built. Roxby Downs supports the mining operations at Olympic Dam, our largest copper and uranium mine, and houses its workers and their families. The median value of a house in Roxby Downs is about $405 000, which is almost the same as a house in Adelaide. However, the average annual growth rate over 10 years in Roxby Downs is 14.4 per cent, compared with Adelaide's 10.4 per cent. This means that the median house price in the remote purpose-built town has increased by 4 per cent more than Adelaide's median house price every year, on average for the last 10 years.

Can such growth continue? Again, we need to look at the cause of the growth. While growth in Roxby Downs has come to a standstill in the last few years, the reason for this is the slowdown in demand for copper. The mine owners are conducting feasibility studies to turn Olympic Dam into a huge open-cut mine and this alone will generate hundreds of new jobs. These workers have nowhere else to live but in Roxby Downs.

To assess the future potential of such mining towns, you should compare information on the expected life of the mine with the expected demand for the minerals it produces. The Chinese and Indian economies are growing strongly, and their demand for our mineral resources (such as aluminium, copper, iron ore, lead, nickel, tin and zinc) is on the rise.

There are other opportunities for investors who want to get in on the ground floor. Demand for uranium will rise if and when the world's economies look to alternative methods of producing electricity, of which nuclear reactors are a cost-effective and efficient source. Australia has a two-uranium-mine policy, which limits our exports, but in the face of international pressure could be obliged to allow export of uranium from its other known deposits, which are the largest in the world.

**Are mining towns right for you?**

If you are unsure about whether to invest in a mining town, take a look at the following list of pros and cons:

⇒ The initial outlay of deposit, stamp duty and legal fees is 10 per cent to 25 per cent of purchase price.

⇒ You will have the ongoing expenses of loan repayments and higher than average maintenance.

⇒ Little expertise and experience are needed apart from knowing which are the best areas to select.

⇒ The duration of investment can be from two to 10 years.

⇒ The risk is low in expanding mine areas and developing ports.

⇒ Rental return can be from 6 per cent to more than 10 per cent if the mining company leases property.

⇒ Capital growth can be the highest in Australia.

# Investments that pay for themselves

Wouldn't it be fantastic to buy an investment property, borrowing most of the purchase price, and then watch it pay for itself from the rent you receive? It seems hard to believe when interest rates are about 6.5 per cent to 7 per cent and rental returns average just 4.5 per cent. Yet, there are many areas that deliver far higher rental yields than this and the tax benefits work in your favour, because each dollar you pay in interest and expenses is offset against each dollar you receive in rent. If your net rental income is greater than your interest bill, you will be taxed only on the extra rental income. You can then use this money to pay off the principal of your loan. Every year puts you further in front because rents tend to rise, while your repayments do not unless interest rates rise, but interest rates can also fall.

Let's take a look at an example. Say you buy an investment property for $350000. You pay a 10 per cent deposit of $35000 and borrow the remaining $315000. Table 5.1 shows how your balance can go from negative to positive in four years.

Table 5.1: from negative to positive gearing in four years

| Year | Rent | Interest | Return | Balance |
|------|------|----------|--------|---------|
| 2010 | $18200 | $20500 | −$2300 | −$2300 |
| 2011 | $20020 | $20500 | −$480 | −$2780 |
| 2012 | $22022 | $20500 | +$1522 | −$1258 |
| 2013 | $23123 | $20500 | +$2623 | +$1365 |

Source: Residex and Australian National Library Archives.

As you can see, four years after buying the property, the rent covers the repayments and can then pay off the loan.

Conventional wisdom says that the highest rental returns are found in the lowest socioeconomic areas, and that higher rental returns compensate for lower capital growth. However, I have found that the highest rents are found in areas where rent is subsidised either by governments or private companies.

Sometimes the subsidy is, in effect, paid by the renters, when groups of renters combine to share the rent. You can obtain high rental yield in many different locations and types of dwellings, so the choice is not so much where to obtain the highest rental yield, but what sort of investment purchase suits your planned results and situation. High rental yields can be obtained from larger houses, older units, former housing commission houses and modern inner-city units.

## Large houses and units

Large houses and units are popular for renting to student group households, both in the major cities and regional centres where there are tertiary institutions. Similar accommodation can be rented to backpackers and as short-term holiday rentals in tourist destinations. Workers in mining towns look for the same styles of accommodation and overseas students seek similar rentals in inner-city precincts or near their university. It can be extremely financially rewarding—three or more renters in a group household will generate far more rent than one family in the same dwelling, and in larger houses can even double the rental yield you might expect. This will only work if you live in the same town and can effect minor maintenance yourself or appoint a manager to look after affairs in the dwelling on your behalf.

Location is the prime consideration, as these renters will generally not have any transport of their own and rely on proximity to all the facilities they need. The exceptions are mining workers and in many cases the lease is arranged on their behalf by the mining company, who will also guarantee the rental payments for the period of the lease. These investments can also provide good capital growth, as they are popular with investors.

# Former housing commission houses and older units

Low-income areas where many residents are on welfare and receive rental assistance also generate high yields, as the government relies on investors to provide the private accommodation that it cannot. Many of these are old public housing estates where much of the housing has passed into private hands. Over time, the houses are refurbished and the area can change quite dramatically into a desirable location. Most of the housing commission estates that were developed in the 1960s and 1970s on what was then the city suburban fringe have experienced the growth of suburbs around them. Many are now in middle-distance suburbs with a full range of facilities and services.

Another group that is forced to rent is made up of newly arrived overseas migrants and their choices are based on location and price. They prefer middle-distance units or houses in areas close to services and transport. Price is an issue, so they will take up the cheaper rental properties that are available, which means older style units and former housing commission properties. Rental yields for such dwellings can be extremely high, as these renters have little choice in where they live or what they pay.

# Modern inner-city units

Generation Y households prefer city living in areas where the facilities and services they desire to maintain their lifestyles are close at hand. The proliferation of high-rise apartment complexes complete with retail and commercial levels, and recreational facilities such as swimming pools, gymnasiums and barbecue areas, are a direct response to this generation of renters. The essential ingredients are location (close to restaurants, shops, transport and employment) and well-appointed units with spectacular views.

High rental yields and low vacancy rates characterise these units as investments, and often their development leads to the refurbishment of whole precincts, creating a new surge of demand. Up to 50 per cent of these units are investor owned, making this one of the few housing markets where an influx of investors leads to capital growth. The number of local investors is increasing and, according to Australian Bureau of Statistics figures, the amount of housing finance they obtain is nearly 40 per cent of total housing finance. In addition, the number of foreign investors entering the Australian market is rapidly growing and the freeing up of restrictions on their investments enables them to buy up to 100 per cent of units in new development such as Central Park in Sydney and Docklands in Melbourne. There are more than three million generation Y residents in Australia, and as they leave home they are forming about one million new households, mostly in the capital cities. This continual increase in investors and renters will ensure that high-rise unit developments in the heart of the capital cities continue to provide excellent rental returns, even as prices increase.

✦ ✦ ✦

The key is to invest in the type of property suited to ongoing rental demand in that location and avoid investments that fail to satisfy this need. For example, in economic boom times, younger, upwardly mobile business owners and entrepreneurs who want to demonstrate their success will rent extravagant houses or units in highly sought-after areas. Rents in such locations can seem attractive to investors, who are also flush with optimism due to the economic conditions; however, when economic conditions deteriorate, as they always do, these high-flyers quickly move out and return to more affordable accommodation. The proportion of rentals in such areas is much lower than in typical rental suburbs, so there is a dramatic effect on rents in such suburbs and investors take a hammering, both in rental return and the value of these investments.

**Are investments that pay for themselves right for you?**

If you are unsure about whether to invest in a property that pays for itself, take a look at the following list of pros and cons:

⇒ The initial outlay of deposit, stamp duty and legal fees is 10 per cent to 25 per cent of purchase price.

⇒ You will have the ongoing expenses of loan repayments and maintenance for most rentals.

⇒ Little expertise and experience are needed apart from knowing which are the best areas to select.

⇒ The duration of investment can be indefinite.

⇒ The risk is low in fully developed areas located near transport and services.

⇒ The rental return grows steadily from 5 per cent each year.

⇒ Capital growth is low initially and increases over the medium term.

# Consistently high capital growth with low risk

Strange as it may seem, there are some locations that will predictably perform better in terms of capital growth than others. Where are these areas and why do they perform better than others? Even though the long-term average total return of housing tends to even out across the entire housing market, we have seen how this translates into higher capital growth and lower rental returns, or the opposite. When a housing market is in a long phase of good steady growth, this is likely to be experienced in all areas of the market. When these conditions occur, it is much better to buy at the high end of the market (if you can) and go for growth, rather than buying at the low end of the market and achieving higher rental return.

For example, one investor buys a million-dollar house, while another buys one for $100 000. Capital growth of about 10 per cent translates into $100 000 for a million-dollar house, but only $10 000 per year for one valued at $100 000. Even if the rental return for the million-dollar house is only 2 per cent, this results in rent of $20 000 per annum, while the $100 000 house on a 5 per cent rental return results in only $5000 each year. As time goes on, the difference in total return increases while the market stays in growth.

Such overall housing market growth only occurs when conditions favour all segments of the market. At the first-home buyer end of the market, interest rates are low, rents are high and lenders are receptive to first-home buyers. At the high socioeconomic end of the market, business conditions are good, the sharemarket is booming and company profits are high. We witnessed such boom periods on the Gold Coast during the early 1980s and in Perth from 2004 to 2008.

Take a look at figure 5.2, which shows that Perth's property market grew from a median value of $200 000 in July 2002 to $500 000 in just four years. That growth of 250 per cent was evenly spread across the entire market due to the economic conditions brought about by the minerals export boom. An investor whose house at the top end of the market was worth $1 million in 2002 achieved capital growth of $1.5 million. At the other end of the market, the other investor achieved just $150 000.

Figure 5.2: Perth's housing market, 2002 to 2008

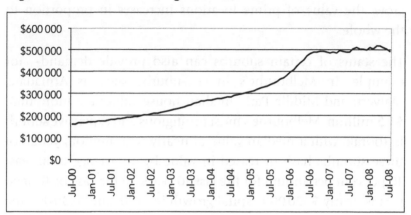

Source: Residex dwelling price indices.

While the economic conditions that produce such good growth are not common, they can be recognised and taken advantage of by investors with sufficient capital to buy at the high end of the market. Growth typically lasts for up to four years, and then comes to an abrupt end, with falls occurring at the low end of the market first, usually because of rising interest rates and unemployment levels. This hides the oncoming correction, because the median price of house sales can still be rising even as falls start to occur at the low end of the market. You can anticipate such corrections by watching the low end of the market, which I explain in chapter 8.

Other properties that will consistently provide better-than-average growth are those located in premium areas. As cities grow, the number of properties at or near beaches, bays or harbours, or with a view or adjacent to parklands, diminishes in proportion to the whole. As a city grows, development occurs along the most highly prized corridors and locations, and suburbs can be established in desirable areas with gaps of bush or farm country in between. It is a bit like people getting on a bus at each stop and occupying the window seats first. When they are all taken, the other seats fill up, but a window seat becoming vacant is immediately snapped up. The property market behaves in the same way and, as cities grow, the value of prime locations increases in proportion to the whole.

The status of certain suburbs can also provide demand — for example, in Melbourne's inner suburbs such as Armadale, Malvern and Middle Park, median house values are more than $1.5 million. Melbourne's most prestigious and expensive suburb is Toorak, with a median value of nearly $2.9 million, yet all of these suburbs have increased in value by an average of at least 10 per cent per annum for the last 10 years. In the case of Toorak, that is nearly $300 000 capital growth in 2010, and $330 000 the year after, and so on. While this will not occur every year, 10 per cent of $3 million is a lot more than 10 per cent of $300 000.

This also applies to units in prestigious suburbs, and those with a harbour or city view, or near a location that is becoming increasingly scarce. It also applies when a desired feature is suddenly added to an otherwise average area. The building of the southern suburban railway line from Perth to Mandurah saw much fruitless speculation in land prices while it was underway, but when the line finally opened it created a surge in house prices of around 20 per cent in Mandurah and other suburbs along the line. Investors who knew this would happen made a tidy profit, because the growth always occurs after the work is finished — in much the same way as we see growth in mining towns when the mine opens and again when it expands. The reason, of course, is the increased demand caused by households wanting to move in. Speculating investors who purchased when the railway line was announced were the losers, unless they were prepared to wait a long time for the growth.

You may think that the most sought-after areas of a town or city are easy to identify because they are the most expensive, but this is not always the case. Undiscovered jewels can be hidden away, waiting to be discovered, and many an investor has struck it rich with such finds. Until recently, some of Sydney's northern beachside suburbs still contained pockets of holiday homes, timber and weatherboard shacks originally occupied only on weekends. There are still a few here and there, but nearly all have been extensively renovated and made their owners a fortune.

There are also some towns in magnificent locations along the eastern and southern coastlines with old housing commission homes, or workers' cottages from a bygone era still untouched. These will slowly disappear one by one, transformed into two-storey 'mansionettes' or colonial restorations, and their prices will skyrocket as a result. The restricted nature of prime locations makes them more and more valuable in relation to the entire housing market and they are the most reliable investments for capital growth over long periods of time.

### Are consistently high-performing areas right for you?

If you are unsure of whether to invest in consistently high-performing areas, take a look at the following list of pros and cons:

⇒ The deposit may be high, but banks are more willing to provide finance.

⇒ Loan repayments are high, but maintenance will be low.

⇒ Little expertise and experience are needed apart from knowing which are the best areas to select.

⇒ The duration of the investment can be indefinite.

⇒ The risk is low and reduces over time.

⇒ The rental return is low, but there is opportunity to lease as executive accommodation.

⇒ Capital growth is regular and the highest of any investment.

# City versus country investments

Some investment advisers will tell you to stick to investing in property in the major cities. They will assure you that, historically, country and regional areas are too risky and the returns are lower. They will remind you that we are an urban society and there has been a drift to the cities, especially by younger people, which has been going on for generations. They will point out that the emergence of road transport as the national carrier has led to the decline of county railway towns and ports, and Australia, especially the southern half, is subject to periodic droughts while the north experiences cyclones that leave rural economies in tatters and regional towns in ruin and decay.

This thinking ignores a fundamental fact about the rural housing market: it is not one market at all. The largest island landmass in the world has great variations in climate and economic performance, and it comprises many different housing markets in the country areas. There are urban areas formed by the growth of towns that act like extensions of their neighbouring capital cites, and there are large regional towns and cities, mining towns, ports, farming towns, tourist meccas, and current and future retirement destinations.

Our state capital cities are coastal and mostly situated in the southern half of the continent, but they are rapidly expanding outwards and in the process creating urban areas that behave like their larger neighbours. For example:

> ➤ Wollongong and the Central Coast outside Sydney (the combined population of these areas is five million people)

> ➤ the Gold Coast, Ipswich and Sunshine Coast outside Brisbane (the combined population of these areas is three million people)

> the Mornington Peninsula and Geelong outside Melbourne (the combined population of these areas is more than four million people).

In fact, price rises of certain types of houses in the capital cities will inevitably ripple though similar housing markets in these suburban outposts. This can create wealth for investors who watch the trends in the capitals, but it can also work the other way. The unit markets on the Gold Coast and Sunshine Coast are very large, comprising about one-quarter of all the units in Queensland, and because they are close to Brisbane they have a powerful effect on that city's unit market prices. When oversupplies occur on the Gold Coast, they tend to have a restraining effect on Brisbane's unit market prices. At the time of writing, oversupply in the Gold Coast unit market means the Brisbane unit market is not a good investment option.

## Large regional towns and cities

Further away from the capital cities there are large regional towns and cities, which at present are too difficult for residents to commute to. This means they are only indirectly affected by capital city housing price movements. Of importance to investors are cities such as Newcastle and Goulburn in New South Wales, Toowoomba in Queensland, or Ballarat and Bendigo in Victoria.

Of even more importance is the fact that, due to the relentless expansion of our capital cities, these regional towns, which are currently around two hours' drive from their capital city, are becoming viewed as possible solutions to the housing shortage in the major cities. They have an abundance of land and little of the infrastructure problems that beset the major cities, providing a combination of urban facilities with the pleasures of living in the country. Housing prices are around half those of similar houses in the capitals and the only disincentive is the need to commute to the capital city for work.

---

**Food for thought**

According to Australian demographic statistics from the ABS, the largest regional cities or areas in Australia include the following:

⇒ the Gold Coast, in Queensland, and Tweed, in New South Wales, which together have a population of 600 000

⇒ Newcastle, in New South Wales, which has a population of 550 000

⇒ Wollongong, in New South Wales, which has a population of 290 000

⇒ the Sunshine Coast, in Queensland, which has a population of 250 000

⇒ Geelong, in Victoria, which has a population of 175 000

⇒ Townsville, in Queensland, which has a population of 172 000

⇒ Cairns, in Queensland, which has a population of 153 000

⇒ Toowoomba, in Queensland, which has a population of 128 000.

---

There are some emerging solutions to this problem, but they will not come into effect until political considerations force governments to act. The construction of fast train networks to these cities, which would significantly reduce the travelling time, is one of the most frequently discussed solutions to the continuing sprawl of our capital cities. Development of these areas so they can provide local employment is another. When it becomes politically expedient to promote them they will start to become a reality.

Investors can take advantage of policy changes and initiatives for regional areas by watching the influence of special-interest parties in parliament as they start to lobby for regional areas, and then waiting for the arrival of the fast train lines, the rollout of a national broadband network, the building of new schools, universities, hospitals and programs to support regional employment. Remember, though, that real growth is dependent on people. Do not be among the first wave of investors who will charge into these towns when new initiatives are announced. Politicians have a way of not keeping promises, or of reducing the cost of meeting them when the political landscape changes. Huge infrastructure projects always take longer and cost more than planned. Wait for the programs that will encourage people to move to these regional cities and buy properties there at that time.

Large parts of rural Australia are subject to periodic droughts and this can put local residential housing markets into a tailspin. Lower production of wool, dairy products, livestock and grains quickly affects the welfare of local industries dependent on them, such as abattoirs, dairies, wineries and canneries, and this then flows into other areas of business. The last drought, which in large parts of Australia went on for well over 10 years, is only just over. Housing markets in the worst areas hardly grew in value during the last five years while growth in other regional areas and capital cities went on unabated.

Figure 5.3 (overleaf) shows the affect drought has had on prices in areas such as the Wimmera in Victoria, the Riverland in South Australia and the Riverina in New South Wales, compared with their capital cities.

## Figure 5.3: capital city growth and drought-affected areas

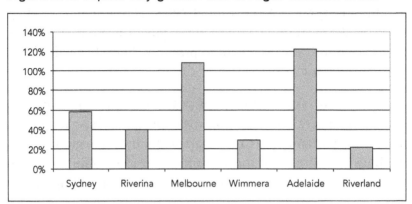

Source: Residex quarterly reports.

With the drought now over, it is not a question of whether housing prices will rise in those regions, but when. The key, once again, is population growth. Some of the towns in the worst areas have actually suffered falls in population as people left to find work elsewhere. Growth in the housing market will begin when employment opportunities return and people move back into the towns in these drought affected areas. There are three important facts about this market for investors:

1   Having lain dormant for so long, prices in these areas are set to catch up price-wise when conditions improve.

2   These areas will provide excellent rental returns once the initial oversupplies are taken up.

3   These areas are extremely affordable. In many towns in the irrigation areas of New South Wales, Victoria and South Australia houses can be bought for under $200 000.

Mining towns and ports form a distinct sector of the country housing market and have been covered separately in this chapter. Another important and highly selective country housing market is resorts and holiday destinations. Although much of the housing demand is seasonal, in many cases there is sufficient ongoing business activity to sustain housing markets when conditions are good. One feature of this market is that when economic conditions are bad, local tourist areas do well, as Australians choose to holiday locally rather than go overseas. The variable nature of tourism means that such towns are not in themselves good investment areas, but when combined with other activities, such as mining or retirement, they can enhance the potential of the area for investors.

Retirement destinations have traditionally been thought of as high-rise pleasure grounds such as the Gold Coast, but in chapter 4 you saw how and why final homebuyers are likely to choose entirely different areas and when this is likely to start happening. With four million baby boomers approaching retirement, some major fluctuations in the supply and demand ratios will occur both in the suburbs they move from, as well as those they relocate to.

Following are some of the areas boomers will likely move to:

➤ the Central Coast and Hunter Valley, and north and south coast towns in New South Wales close to Sydney or with an airport

➤ the Mornington and Bellarine peninsulas, and east coast and Great Ocean Road towns in Victoria

➤ the Sunshine Coast, Mackay and the Whitsundays in Queensland

➤ the Fleurieu and Yorke peninsulas, Murray River Towns, Penola and Ceduna in South Australia

➤ Bunbury, Busselton and Albany in Western Australia

➤ Wynyard, Somerset, Ulverstone, George Town, Dodges Ferry and Huonville in Tasmania.

Not all baby boomers will move, and some may buy holiday homes and alternate between city and country living, but the groundswell will grow and the weight of their numbers will dramatically alter the types of services and facilities on offer in their destinations. It will be a very different situation in towns where there are already large numbers of retirees, because as these residents move to retirement homes and hospices, there will be an oversupply of houses in these areas. These areas may be able to cope with the demographic changes, but investors should be wary of towns and cities with a high median age, such as the Gold Coast and Hervey Bay in Queensland, and Byron Bay in New South Wales.

---

### Which area is right for you—the city or the country?

If you are unsure about whether to invest in the city or the country, take a look at the following comparison of features:

⇒ The initial outlay in a country town is usually much lower than in the city.

⇒ The ongoing expenses can be higher in the country due to shortage of skilled tradespeople.

⇒ Little expertise or experience are needed in the recommended country areas.

⇒ The duration of investment in the country can vary according to local return patterns.

⇒ The risk is very low in the recommended country areas.

⇒ The rental returns in many country areas are likely to fall more quickly than in capital cities if economic conditions deteriorate.

⇒ Capital growth in many country areas is likely to be higher than in capital cities over the next few years.

---

Over the next few years there will be a much greater focus on regional development by the government and increasing numbers of retirees moving to retirement locations. As a result, country markets in many areas are set to enter a boom period and destroy the maxim that rural areas provide higher rent and lower growth while the city housing market does the opposite.

# Climate change: the bad, the ugly and the good

Climate change presents both challenges and opportunities for investors. It is a whole new ball game, but the effects of climate change are already starting to place pressures on some housing markets and present opportunities for others. Even if this was not the case it would not matter because it is the perception of climate change that is important. The perception is what may make buyers reluctant to buy in low-lying coastal areas because of the fear of rising ocean levels. It is the perception of climate change that may have an effect on building regulations, forcing builders to construct green houses (that is, energy-efficient houses made with sustainable building materials). Some people may even use this perception to their own advantage. Let's take a look at what effect it has had so far.

## The bad

Over the last 50 years the average maximum temperature over much of southern Australia has been rising. At the same time, the incidence of low rainfall has been increasing. During the prolonged drought that gripped much of Australia from 2001 to 2010, this combination of trends led to a drastic lowering of dam levels in southern cities and high water restrictions. Catastrophic bushfires caused widespread loss of stock and houses, and water allocations along the Darling and Murray rivers were slashed and many farmers faced ruin. The cause was the rise in maximum temperatures, which was warming the continental landmass and driving the rain delivering cold fronts further south, even during the winter months. As a consequence, rain often missed the mainland altogether.

Towns in the irrigated areas of the south, such as the Riverland and Riverina, went into decline as conditions worsened. The economic decline extended from the wheat belt in Western Australia, to the grape-growing regions of South Australia, the dairy and horticultural localities of Victoria, and up through New South Wales and into western Queensland. In many towns, the exodus of unemployed workers caused falls in population, leaving then with an oversupply of housing stock. Not only did farmers suffer, because tourism declined in areas that relied on a steady supply of water and on water for recreational activities. That this was due to climate change is beyond doubt, yet some locals in the worst-affected areas still insisted that it was all part of a cycle.

This long-term drying up of vast areas around the world has been occurring since the end of the last Ice Age and resulted in the creation and growth of deserts since then. To see this as a cycle is to misunderstand the nature of climate change, which is not that we are making the earth warmer, but that we are changing the world's weather patterns in unpredictable ways. At the time of writing, one manifestation of this change is the drying up of much of central and southern Australia.

## The ugly

What of the ugly side to climate change? Surely it must be the way that it has been used as a cause to the point that many believe the world's oceans will rise and swallow whole areas of low-lying cities. Beyond the rise caused by the expansion of the water in the oceans as they get slightly warmer, the only real way in which water levels can rise is by a melting of the ice sheets in Antarctica or the Greenland ice cap. While there is no doubt that the Greenland ice cap is receding, even allowing for an increase in the rate of its annual net melt, it will take hundreds of years to cause any significant rise in sea levels. The Antarctic ice cap and ice sheets are more stable.

All along our coastline, developments are being refused because of climate change. Authorities are withholding permission, claiming that there is future risk for which local councils may be liable. However, this is like banning something now because of a possible problem that may occur hundreds of years from now. Cynics may say that local authorities are using climate change to deter unwelcome developments from their coastlines, in the interests of the current residents. As an investor you need to take the attitude of the council and other local authorities into account. Before purchasing low-lying properties close to ocean activity, bear in mind the possible risk of erosion and storm damage, as tropical storms may increase in intensity and move further south due to climate change.

## The good

Is there any good that climate change is likely to bring investors? Residents of Tasmania will notice a gradual warming of annual temperatures, and less snowfall at lower altitudes. This is already encouraging growers to introduce crops previously thought not suitable to the colder climate of the island state. In particular, the eastern coast, which is protected from the worst of the icy southern weather in winter, may experience milder conditions. It is important to remember that climate change is about trends that take a long time to become apparent. There can be a return to colder weather, and even some bitterly cold years, but the trend will continue.

Another effect of climate change is the lowering of the monsoonal trough, which occurs every summer in the tropics and brings the annual 'big wet' to the north. Whereas cyclones in the past veered away again when they hit the north-west or north-east coastline, as they happen further down they are now continuing across the continent and turn into vast tropical rain depressions, bringing enormous amounts of water into the river systems that eventually run into the Darling and Murray rivers. Dams, lakes and water storages all along this huge river system are refilling and the prospect of a return to prosperity is imminent for growers in the Riverina, the Riverland and towns all along the Murray River system such as Shepparton, Mildura, Leeton, Berri, Loxton, Barmera and Renmark. Watch for the rains in the north, and then invest in such town as the canneries, juicing plants and wineries reopen, and demand for housing surges.

In cities, we are seeing a trend to green housing initiatives, which in part seek to address the problems associated with climate change, such as water shortages and higher electricity consumption charges. These are starting to become politically expedient, and so we may see real benefits for investors, including an increase in demand for green housing.

✦ ✦ ✦

In this chapter we have looked at different areas around Australia with the greatest capital growth or rent potential in both the short and long term. As there are about 12 000 suburbs and towns around Australia, you will have narrowed your search down to just one or two types of areas. In chapter 6 we explore the various investment options available.

# Your investment options

As an investor, you are faced with many options: do you buy a house, a unit or vacant land? Do you invest in an existing property or purchase one off the plan? Do you buy and hold, or do you trade and flip? Do you buy a house and renovate? All of these approaches have their merits at the right time and place, and for the right type of investor. In this chapter I explore all of these options to help you with your investment decision.

## Land, houses or units

How do you decide whether to invest in land, houses or units? You will need to weigh up the pros and cons of each option. Land provides no income, but it does have the maximum potential capital gain. Houses can be renovated and negatively or positively geared, and provide both rent and capital growth. Units offer the least development potential and riskier capital gains, but provide maximum rental return and the best gearing opportunities. To help you choose which is the best investment for your situation, let's look at each of these alternatives.

## Investing in land

Land was once the most significant indicator of social status in Australia. From earliest colonial times, land was granted to ex-convicts to enable them to form a productive role in society. It was also given as a reward for military service and for exploring the hinterland. In some cases, such as the settlement of Melbourne by John Batman, it was bartered from the Indigenous people without approval by the governing authorities. Land was the key to survival, as the early farms were entirely self-sufficient, and was also the path to political power. The right to hold a seat and even to vote in colonial government elections was at first restricted to landowners and only gradually extended to landless tenants. Even into the modern era, only property owners could vote in local government elections and in many states they still have plural votes — that is, one vote per property rather than one vote per resident.

More importantly, land provided the opportunity to become wealthy. Speculation in land followed the discovery and mining of gold, the establishment of ports and the building of railways. Enormous land booms followed the proposed routes of train lines beyond the suburban areas of major cities in the second half of the 19th century, as land was quickly subdivided and put on the market. These were entirely undeveloped plots of land, purchased in the hope that this was where the stations would be located.

During the postwar baby boom years, couples typically bought a block of land in new land developments, and then used the land as security to obtain finance and start building. This led to whole families living in substandard and cramped temporary homes while the house was being built, usually with the entire family helping. At the same time, these subdivisions often had limited access to water and power, while proper sewerage and drainage services arrived years later.

This postwar experience of long delays in services led state governments to engage in major construction projects to provide affordable housing, known generally as housing commissions. It also enabled them to ensure a plentiful supply of labour in the areas where it was most needed — the major manufacturing locations around Sydney, Melbourne and Adelaide, in particular. Entire suburbs were created from the ground up and provided to new households and migrant families on a 'rent now, buy later' arrangement.

Social problems with these developments caused several changes in direction by state governments, which control the sale of Crown land. By the 1960s, land in outer suburban areas was becoming scarce and the cost of development was increasing. Local governments, which had to pay the costs of improving roads and drainage, made it obligatory for subdividers — including the state governments — to provide services before the land was sold, not after. Some states provided suburban land lots on an 'at-cost' basis, but because the demand was far greater than the supply, many conducted land lotteries for newly subdivided Crown land in outer suburban areas. Although thousands of hopeful first-home buyers went into the ballots, only a lucky few were winners. As a result, this policy gave way to a blatant sell-off of Crown land in highly desired areas to the highest bidder. From the days when governments granted land as a reward, things have turned full circle with governments selling Crown land to reward themselves.

The concept of the inherent value of land is what encourages many investors to compare the underlying land value of their investments. This leads them to prefer houses to units, for the reason that the land value per unit is far less than that per house. However, this idea ignores the fact that we buy, sell, value and insure properties for their improved value, not their land value, and that the resale value of any property includes the value of the improvements made.

In the case of units, the value of the improvements varies considerably from one unit in a block to another. One may have a spectacular view and the unit next door may not. To measure the value of a unit in terms of its share of the land on which the unit block is built is flawed, as it ignores the value of the attributes that have real value while the unit exists. This is why strata titles for units treat the land, areas controlled by the body corporate and individual units as a legal entity. In order for an entire block to be pulled down and redeveloped, there must be a consensus among the titleholders acting as the body corporate over the value not only of the entire block, but of each unit holder's share in that value. It is this proven potential value that determines the land value of the block as a whole and explains why the land value of a block of units has a much higher value than that of a neighbouring one only approved for houses.

This brings us back to the inherent value of land as an investment. The scams mentioned in chapter 3 mostly involve unimproved land, because the potential for fraud is greater and the value is comparatively low, making it easier to find gullible buyers. There are fewer opportunities for fraud with land that has been subdivided and improved to the point where roads and footpaths are laid, and sewerage, drainage and other services are available. There is also a hidden danger for investors in land. There are numerous cases of overdevelopment in rural areas and regional resort towns, where developers have overestimated the demand and estates have remained in a semi-dormant existence for years.

**Food for thought**

Never buy land on impulse. One couple I know found out the hard way what can happen if you buy with your heart and not with your head:

'We fell in love with the Gold Coast on our honeymoon and before we left, put down the deposit for land in a hinterland development. Because of the repayments, the bank wouldn't give us any more finance and we couldn't buy the house we wanted. Not only did we have to make the repayments, we had to pay rent and couldn't sell the land because we owed more than it was worth. By the time we sold the land the value of houses in Melbourne had gone up so much we could no longer buy where we had planned to.'

Developers like to subdivide and market residential land estates in regional areas as there is an abundance of land. They offer inducements such as options to buy, which give the rural owner some badly needed cash in times of drought or economic downturn, while enabling the developer to select the best time to exercise the option. It is also far more difficult for prospective buyers to evaluate what the worth of such blocks of land is, as there have not been any sales, only purchases. The value of land is what you can sell it for, not what you pay the developers. Some land developers offer finance packages to encourage buyers.

The first rule of buying land for investment is its location. You should only ever buy land in developed areas where it is already scarce because the days of quick profits from land sales are long gone and today buyers overwhelmingly choose to buy and build, or buy existing dwellings. Only consider land that has some differentiating attribute, such as potential ocean views or rezoning potential.

The point of investing in land is to obtain a better return than you would from houses or units and this can only come from your capital gain. Land does not provide you with an ongoing return, only with expenses such as keeping your land scrub and vermin free and paying council rates. Making repayments on finance for an asset that provides no return is folly when houses and units provide good returns. Your eventual capital gain is offset by the value of the repayments you have made and you have foregone the revenue that could have been made from an investment in a house or unit. Buying land for investment is something only for those with knowledge about the potential for rapid price rises in a particular area.

## Investing in units

At the other end of the risk spectrum are units, which offer high rental returns and can also provide good capital growth. There is little development potential, as the development has been completed. Opportunities for renovation are also usually limited to cosmetic improvements of the interior.

Units are becoming a popular form of rental accommodation for new households and overseas arrivals, while an increasing number of couples without children and retirees prefer buying and living in units rather than houses. This is largely because our inner cities have been transformed in recent years, with old commercial and industrial areas, wharves and warehouses redeveloped into desirable living precincts. It is high-density unit blocks that have made this possible. They have brought million-dollar views and a range of living facilities previously available only to the wealthy into the reach of generation Y renters and generation X couples on professional incomes. These developments combine ground-floor retail areas with several commercial levels, and provide recreational facilities such as swimming pools, gymnasiums, barbecue and entertainment areas in the one block. They make unit living desirable and as such they offer investors enormous opportunities. Table 6.1 shows that the proportion of units to houses in our major capital cities is increasing.

Table 6.1: the proportion of units to houses in the major cities

| City | 2000 | 2005 | 2010 |
|------|------|------|------|
| Sydney | 85% | 95% | 110% |
| Melbourne | 50% | 60% | 70% |
| Brisbane | 20% | 25% | 35% |
| Perth | 10% | 15% | 25% |

Source: Building Approvals and Commencements, Australian Bureau of Statistics.

You can buy a unit for far less than a similar style of house, making units an excellent first investment. There is far less that can go wrong, so your maintenance bill will be lower than it would be for a house, and the body corporate looks after all external maintenance and improvements. This is why so many overseas investors buy units, especially off-the-plan developments, because the property and building managers will look after everything. If you do not have the time or desire to get involved with such matters, then unit investment is perfect.

The most important consideration with units is their location. If they are in desirable urban centres, or near major transport hubs or recreation areas, they are easy to rent and provide excellent rental returns. If you buy in the right area, you will find that your investment becomes positively geared very quickly, with your rental receipts becoming greater than the interest you are paying for the loan. Not only will your unit rarely be vacant for very long between rentals, but you can increase the rent each time in accordance with market conditions.

Even though units are traditionally a low-maintenance investment, problems with units can occur at two periods. The first is a few years after construction, when any shortcuts taken by the builders start to become visible. The exteriors will feature rust and watermarks, poor paint jobs will begin to become apparent and cracks may show in hastily completed plastered and rendered surfaces. The second is when the effects of poor building practices become apparent and cause real problems for the owners and tenants. Many units constructed during the 1960s and 1970s in some suburban council areas are starting to show signs of concrete cancer and plumbing breakdowns that seriously affect their continued viability as accommodation. The best remedy for prospective purchasers is to insist on a full building inspection, look at recent meeting minutes of the body corporate to see what has been discussed and find out how much is in the sinking fund to cover such contingencies.

## Investing in houses

Houses provide greater potential for capital growth than units and, even though house rents on average may be higher than units, they provide a lower rental yield in return. Each house occupies an amount of land and so the value of houses is aligned with the value of the land area that they are located on. Where developed land is in short supply, good growth can be expected. With apartments, however, a huge capacity still exists to build more, as low-density homes can be knocked down and replaced with large unit blocks. The land content attached to homes also means that they are less risky investments and therefore better suited to cautious investors. The differences in price and rent between units and houses can be seen in table 6.2.

Table 6.2: unit prices and rents versus house prices and rents

| City | Median unit price | Percentage of median house price | Median rent of unit | Percentage of median rented house |
|---|---|---|---|---|
| Sydney | $468 000 | 70% | $440 | 88% |
| Melbourne | $451 000 | 76% | $350 | 93% |
| Darwin | $422 000 | 81% | $440 | 81% |
| Canberra | $420 000 | 80% | $410 | 89% |
| Perth | $410 000 | 83% | $350 | 95% |
| Brisbane | $368 000 | 79% | $350 | 92% |
| Adelaide | $310 000 | 76% | $270 | 84% |
| Hobart | $284 000 | 74% | $260 | 76% |

Source: Residex Quarterly Reports.

The value of a house can also be improved to a far greater extent than is possible with units. You can paint the walls, remodel the kitchen or bathroom, but, ultimately, the unit constrains you by its internal space. You can do all this with houses, but a house can also be extended outwards and upwards, so you can create more living space and additional rooms. You can also paint or clad the exterior walls, redo the roof, add a pool, put in decking and an outdoor entertainment area, and landscape the garden. Everything you do to improve the liveability, appearance and functionality of a house adds to its value.

Investment in a house usually requires higher capital investment, but as units become the only available option for those wishing to live in the most sought-after areas in our capital cites, they are becoming more desirable. The price differential between units and houses has been steadily falling, and the rent generated from units compared with houses has been steadily rising. This is why both the capital growth of units has been higher than houses as well as the rental returns. Houses have always been considered the safer investment, but perhaps we are seeing not just a change in the pattern, but an irreversible trend in our housing market of huge importance to investors.

✦ ✦ ✦

In summary, land investors should obtain good capital growth and only speculate with funds they will not need for other investments. Houses offer the best option for renovation and land improvement and this should be considered before you buy, not after. For investors not able to keep an eye on their investment, or wishing to renovate or refurbish, units offer the most suitable investment option. Of most importance is to research the area and assess its potential for further development, and for overdevelopment. Select units that have a special feature, such as a view or particular location, and only buy units that have been sold at least once before, so that you can measure their real worth and inspect the quality of workmanship that went into them.

**Which is right for you: land, units or houses?**

If you are unsure about whether to invest in land, units or houses, take a look at the following list of pros and cons:

⇒ The initial outlay is lowest for units and highest for land.

⇒ The ongoing expenses are lowest for land and highest for houses.

⇒ Land is for short-term capital gain, units are for long-term rental return.

⇒ The risk is high with land and low with houses.

⇒ The rental return is good from houses, but better from units.

⇒ Capital growth can be obtained from all three options, depending on the location and timing.

# Flipping, trading and predatory buying

Many exponents of residential property investment promote strategies such as property flipping and property trading. These are not investment schemes in the sense that you will gain from long-term capital growth or returns from rent. The exponents claim that you will gain from a quick increase in the value of the property derived from buying off the plan with minimal outlay or manipulating vendors using predatory buying techniques. These schemes and techniques do not require you to do much more than buy below market value and sell at market value. The main drawback from such schemes is that they rely on almost immediate growth in the value of the property. If this does not occur, you are in trouble.

Flipping is the process of buying at the lowest possible price, such as at the earliest stages of a new property development when the developer is keen to get some runs on the board. You then hope that the price of the property has increased before you need to settle, which for some large unit developments can be more than a year. If prices have increased sufficiently in the area, you can take the increased value as profit by selling before the unit is completed.

Trading is the process of finding bargains in need of a simple makeover and buying for the lowest possible price. Once some cosmetic improvements have been made, you put the property back on the market and profit from the sale.

While these strategies are not in themselves unethical, they can involve questionable practices such as predatory buying. This is the practice of finding properties that must be sold, no matter what the price. They may be deceased estates, divorce settlements, elderly owners moving to retirement accommodation with no idea of the value of their property or simply uninformed and gullible owners. Perhaps the owners have to relocate to another city or are in financial difficulty. They may have started a renovation that they cannot afford to finish. Predatory buyers trawl property listings and make low offers for every property that appears on the basis that someone somewhere will not get a better offer and they will accept.

Predatory buying derives its profit not so much from any increase in the property's value as it does from the loss suffered by the person selling the property. You are profiting because of the unfortunate circumstances of the person who is selling the property. There are important financial reasons why this approach can fail. Areas where properties are going on the market because of problems with repayments are usually economically depressed areas. Local businesses may have closed, unemployment is up and household income is down. Such areas are unlikely to provide any prospects for capital growth and may be about to fall in value. Buying in these areas goes against the very concept of the sound investment strategies explained in this book.

As informed investors shun these areas, many of the buyers in the market for such properties are predatory buyers who end up competing among themselves and defeating the purpose of the whole exercise. While it is good practice to buy at not more than the real value of a property, it is also crucial to buy in areas where prices are about to rise significantly. Buying in distressed areas can result in a fall in the property's value a year or two down the track.

The other problem with buying such properties is that they are nearly always going to be in need of immediate repair because the owners have been unable or unwilling to maintain the property. This means you will have to spend some time and money on renovations and improvements whether you want to or not, and there is no guarantee that the price will rise significantly as a result. Some deceased estates may be knock-down jobs, while distressed sales are usually run down and, in some cases, have been deliberately vandalised.

It is far more important to buy in the best area at the right price, than it is to buy in a bad area for the best price. I would recommend a sound property for a fair price that is easily rented with good capital growth prospects rather than a bargain-basement priced property that may be impossible to rent, will require substantial improvement and could result in no capital growth.

**Is flipping or trading right for you?**

If you are unsure about whether to try flipping or trading property, take a look at the following list of pros and cons:

⇒ The initial outlay is limited to the deposit.

⇒ There are no ongoing expenses beyond cosmetic improvements.

⇒ Expertise and experience are needed to find properties and negotiate prices.

⇒ The duration of the investment is short.

⇒ There is risk that you could lose money if prices fall.

⇒ The only return is on the increase in price.

⇒ If you hold the property for less than a year, you pay full capital gains tax.

# Renovating

Renovation may seem like a sure-fire way to achieve high returns quickly, but it can have many hidden dangers. For every success story you may read about there will be many more disasters, hiding behind captions such as 'Partially renovated, owner says sell'. When these half-renovated properties are sold, it is invariably for less than their market value because most buyers, who are owner-occupiers, want a finished house to live in. They shun properties with unfinished rooms or piles of dirt and bricks in the front yard. So, what went wrong? The prospective renovators who purchased the property with high hopes left disillusioned and disappointed with their experience, and probably have lost quite a bit of money as well. Before you think about an extensive renovation, even before you look for a suitable property, consider the following question: do you have the time?

Even if you are proposing to use contractors to do much of the work, you will still need to be involved in some basic work to save costs and time. It is pointless taking on such an obligation if your personal or work commitments make this difficult. Assuming that time will make itself available is a huge mistake, because the work will take up more time than you expect and something else will have to suffer — it could be your employment, your friends or, even worse, your relationship. Many renovations have failed because of the stress they have placed on partners, which has forced the renovator to make the ultimate choice, in order to preserve the relationship.

If time is on your side, you need the appropriate skills. These include a wide and varied assortment of building skills such as carpentry, bricklaying, cement rendering, plastering, painting and joinery. Although electrical, plumbing and gas-fitting jobs should only be done by licensed tradespeople, you will need some knowledge of these trades to understand in advance what needs to be done, how long it will take and how much it will cost, before you call in the experts. Then you need to correctly estimate and budget for or borrow enough money to cover the work. This is where most renovation projects go horribly wrong, because they invariably cost more than initially estimated and one problem seems to lead to another. Unless your contingency plan covers unexpected costs and delays, an inability to meet bills and repayments can quickly kill your enthusiasm or, even worse, force your lender to take action.

If you are planning to do most or all of the work yourself, then it is essential to live nearby the property or even in it. Living in a property being renovated brings considerable tax advantages, as you will not have to pay capital gains tax. On the other hand, bumping into piles of timber in the night, taking cold showers and eating off dust-covered crockery does nothing for a relationship.

---

### Food for thought

Here is one success story of a couple who bought the right property in the right area, renovated and made a tidy profit:

'We bought an old two-bedroom corrugated-iron shack for $450 000 — it was definitely the worst in the street and one of the worst in Leichhardt. The council wouldn't let us alter the facade, so we left it cottage-style at the front. We spent 18 months hard work and $200 000 extending the back and renovating the front into a four-bedroom, two-bathroom brick residence while we lived in it. The property went for auction at $1.25 million, giving us a tax-free profit of $600 000. We are now doing the same with a run-down terrace in Camperdown.'

---

Depending on the size and scope of the renovation, you made need local council approval, and this can involve delays and problems with neighbours. In many older suburban areas, councils are increasingly conscious of the aesthetics of renovations, how they may affect the appearance of an area. Facades must be preserved; there are height and boundary restrictions and population density limits. Failure to check on these before you start can be disastrous to your plans. It is a good idea to consult your local council's register of renovations approved in recent years and those successfully objected to and take a look at them. This will give you an insight into council thinking and also may provide you with some innovative ideas.

Always check your title documents for easements and covenants, as building a pergola over a drainage easement could result in you having to pull it down again at your own cost. Check with your neighbours before proceeding—they may not object to the renovation in principle, but they may dislike the building activity itself, because of the interference to their lifestyle caused by the noise and building activities. There have been extreme cases of disputes going to court and resulting in long-running neighbourhood feuds. Although this is unlikely, keeping the neighbours informed and on-side provides you with many unexpected benefits, such as water when yours is turned off and power when yours is disconnected. At the very least, you may receive a hot cup of coffee when both are unavailable to you.

Always check the credentials of subcontractors and builders. Get written quotes for both the cost and expected duration of the work, including materials. Ask for references from them if they are unknown to you. Make sure you have estimated all your costs and the time it will take to complete all the work. This will almost always cost more and take longer than you anticipated, so allow 10 per cent on top for such emergencies. Also, make sure you have access to adequate savings or finance before you start, and that you have local council approval and checked whether it is required.

## Do your homework

All of this is usually contained in renovation guides and courses, but there is something far more important that is seldom if ever covered. When renovating for profit the most important question to ask is, 'Will the renovations add considerably to the sale price?' If the finished property is not worth significantly more than when you bought it, you have wasted your time and money. You need to know not just how much the renovation will cost, but how much it will lift the value of the property. In dealing with the problem of the estimated added value, most experts will advise you to look at similar properties that have been renovated in the area and the increase in value this has created. This assumes that you already own the property that you intend to renovate, but surely the right time to do your research is before you buy, not after.

Your research should start with selecting the right suburbs. Newer suburban areas have virtually no added value potential from renovations. The houses will tend to be slight variations on a theme based on the demographics of the households living in them. The homes have recently been built to cater for the needs of these households, all of which are fairly similar, so adding a garage or granny flat will not increase the home's value beyond the cost of the improvement. It is entirely different with older suburbs, particularly where the household demographics vary considerably.

A suburb containing a mix of Federation-style single-fronted workers' terraces, two-storey Victorian terraces and a smattering of colonial originals will contain a wide variety of households, such as postwar migrant couples, young professionals and wealthy families. These older suburbs will provide the best opportunities for renovation, because of the huge price difference between the various styles and condition of the homes they contain.

Select the best suburbs by the range and variety of dwellings in the suburb, by your purchase price options, and the local council's requirements and restrictions on renovation. Look for new listings in those suburbs that appear to meet your criteria for renovation potential. If you are seeking to refurbish only, then select run-down dwellings of larger than average size. If you are planning to add a room or extend, look for properties with a lower than average number of rooms for the area and sufficient land size to allow for redevelopment.

You need to correctly estimate the value that your improvements will add to the property's sale price. Although you can compare sale prices for similarly renovated properties in the area as many experts suggest, the best way to do this is to look at all the properties in the street and compare their values from lowest to highest. The greater the range and the closer your selected property is to the bottom of that range, the higher your potential for capital gain. This is because every property in a street has a value that bears a relationship to every other property. If you purchase a property at the low end of the street's value and renovate it so it has the attributes and appearance of those at the high value end, it will take on the value of those properties.

Let's say you buy a three-bedroom dwelling in a street with a line of three-bedroom terraces that are identical in appearance. If you renovate this property by adding another bedroom, it will not rise in value as much as it would if you renovated a similar house in a street where there was a range of two-, three- and four-bedroom houses.

There are tools that can help you to look at the range of properties and prices quickly and easily. Google maps and street view will give you a good idea of the range of properties in a street. You can obtain free price estimates or last sale prices from <www. myrp.com.au> or <www.findmeahome.com.au> for properties in a street. Some reports, such as the Residex Right Price report, provide the street price range for any residential property.

Let's take a look at an example. Say you are looking to buy and renovate a house in a street that has a mix of two-, three- and four-bedroom houses. The price range of the properties is as follows:

| | | |
|---|---|---|
| Two-bedroom houses | $300 000 | $450 000 |
| Three-bedroom houses | $600 000 | $750 000 |
| Four-bedroom houses | $800 000 | $950 000 |

If you were to buy a two-bedroom house in this street for $300 000, spend $200 000 on renovations, including adding two more bedrooms, the value of the property would increase to about $800 000. After deducting the cost of the renovations, this leaves you with a potential profit of $300 000.

### Is renovating properties right for you?

If you are unsure whether renovating is the right option for you, take a look at the following list of pros and cons:

⇒ The initial outlay is high, and it is prudent to minimise borrowing.

⇒ The ongoing expenses will be high, and probably more than budgeted.

⇒ Expertise and experience are needed.

⇒ The duration of the investment can be a year or two, but should not be longer.

⇒ The risk is low if property is in the right location and you have the skills.

⇒ The rental return is nil.

⇒ Capital growth can be extremely high, and there is no capital gains tax if you live in the property while renovating.

If you are investing interstate, you simply may not have the desire or ability to renovate or refurbish. You may not want to engage in the risky practices of property flipping or trading and only want a secure long-term investment with minimum risk and outlay. Let's take a look at the best options for hands-off investors.

# Buying off the plan

Nothing could be easier than buying off the plan. The development is only just underway and your purchase is secured by payment of a deposit, which in some cases can be covered as a bond, so there is virtually no up-front cost. Settlement may be up to a year away or even longer, and as prices rise in the mean time, you can sell before settlement and make a tidy profit by flipping something you never really owned. Or, you can settle, rent out the property and watch your equity grow. There are savings in stamp duty, especially if you choose to live in the property for a while, and new properties attract high depreciation allowances with considerable tax benefits when rented out as investments.

However, there are several problems with this scenario, none of which the developers will share with you. Investing in residential property normally bring four parties together — the owner, the lenders, the tenant and the property manager — each of whom plays a part. Buying off the plan introduces another player into the mix — the developer. It is essential to conduct research on the developer — take a look at the developer's previous developments and talk to the owners. Make sure that your deposit is held in a trust fund and not the developer's pockets, so that if the developer goes bankrupt you do not lose your deposit.

Buying off the plan involves putting a deposit down on a property that is still to be completed. You agree to a price in today's terms, and settlement occurs once the home has been completed. From the developer's perspective this is advantageous, reducing the risk he is taking, as the developer has buyers even before the property exists.

For buyers there can be benefits too, because the property is priced in today's terms. Settlement is delayed until completion, so there is potential for good capital returns if housing prices increase while the property is being built. The delayed settlement also means that you have time to save before the final payment is due. As a result you may need to borrow less. Many off-the-plan unit developers will guarantee rents for a period of time, which you can offset against the loan repayments.

## Is buying off the plan right for you?

If you are unsure whether buying off the plan is the right option for you, take a look at the following pros and cons:

⇒ The initial outlay can be low, as the deposit can be paid sometimes as a bond.

⇒ The ongoing expenses are low, as a unit should require no improvements.

⇒ Expertise and experience are needed to buy at the right price in the right area.

⇒ The duration of the investment can be long or short term.

⇒ The risk is high, particularly in times of economic uncertainty.

⇒ Rental return is high, and can be guaranteed for some years by the developer.

⇒ Capital growth may be low initially due to oversupply.

The issues with buying off the plan are that the final version of the unit may not be quite what you expected. Due to cost blowouts, the developer may have resorted to inferior materials and below standard subcontractors, so that promised fittings and features are reduced in quality or missing altogether. There may be optimistic overdevelopment creating the potential for negative growth or at least price stagnation for several years. You have signed a contract that covers the price you agreed on, not what the unit is worth if prices change. Rental guarantees can be a trap as well, because they will all expire at the same time, creating a glut of vacancies in the same area, which can result in desperate owners signing tenancy agreements for far less than current rentals in the area. Off-the-plan investments suit those who are interstate or overseas investors, as maintenance will be minimal and rent is assured for some time.

# What sort of income and lifestyle do you want in retirement?

How can you achieve a reliable and secure income, as well as the opportunity to use some of the profit taken from capital growth without running down your asset base? The secret is to run your investment portfolio through several phases, initially using rent, income and capital growth to borrow against further investment properties, and then increasing equity as you approach retirement to derive a steady and healthy income from rental returns.

You will need some start-up capital to begin your investment journey. In chapter 2 I mentioned the importance of balancing your investment portfolio in accordance with the economic conditions, but it is most important to build cash reserves quickly. There are promoters of 'rent-to-buy' schemes and so-called shared-equity arrangements, which enable you to get a foot in the property investment door, but you may have no legal protection with these operators. If the agreement states that you are technically renting and the operator holds the legal title to the property, you have no legal comeback if something goes wrong — for example, if you are unable to make the payments — or the operator has to sell the property for other reasons.

Be very wary of such schemes. There are lenders who will finance up to 100 per cent of the purchase price of a property, but no-one gets something for nothing. You will be paying a premium interest rate, either now or later, and this also applies to honeymoon rates for first-home buyers — the cost is built into the arrangement, so you will be paying more later.

Another option for raising finance is investing in the share-market — but only if it is rising. If you are a first-home buyer and planning to live in the house and renovate, take advantage of the government's saving schemes for first-home buyers. Most property investors start by buying a property to live in and using all their spare income to build equity. A better idea is to use your spare income to renovate, in which case you should buy a property that meets the requirements listed on page 130. It may not be your preferred choice, but that does not matter, because your intention is to sell.

You can buy an investment property while renting — indeed, the earlier you start, the earlier you will achieve your goals. The most important thing about your first investment property is to build your borrowing power. You can use the increased equity in a home to refinance at any time, so the higher the growth the better. Choose one of the areas I have discussed for maximum short-term capital growth, combined with a reasonable rental return to offset against the interest payments. Have your property's value reassessed frequently (I explain how to do so in chapter 8). Borrow as much as you can, bearing in mind your current and future income and personal security. Fluctuations in interest rates do not really matter, because any increase in interest rates makes it harder for owner-occupiers to borrow, so rental demand and prices go up accordingly. This is, of course, assuming that you have purchased in a high rental demand area.

As soon as you can, buy another house or unit in a high growth potential area. Use as much of your income and rent as you can to repay debt and gain equity. As soon as you have sufficient deposit funds, that is the time to buy again. The crucial difference between this approach and those of many advisers is that you will be buying in the best-possible areas, and by now you will have realised what a huge difference this can make.

The benefit of buying in the right place at the right time can be seen in table 6.3. By buying in the right area you will have increased your capital by $100 000 compared with the capital city median.

Table 6.3: buying in the right place at the right time

| Year | Capital city median | Your area median |
|------|---------------------|------------------|
| 1 | $370 000 | $270 000 |
| 2 | $395 000 | $310 500 |
| 3 | $430 000 | $364 000 |
| 4 | $440 000 | $440 000 |

This method of buying in the best areas also ensures that you minimise your risk, as you are investing in the areas of greatest demand. When you have reached a point where your income from rent is at the amount you want as retirement income, it is time to recycle your investment portfolio. Each year sell one property that has achieved the highest growth and buy one at a similar price for its rental return potential. After doing this with your entire portfolio, you will have converted your investments into the highest providers of income that they can be. At this point it is time to enjoy your retirement and let your property managers look after affairs for you.

**Is a retirement plan based on property right for you?**

If you are unsure whether basing your retirement plan on the income derived from your property investments is the right option for you, take a look at the following pros and cons:

⇒ You will need expertise or advice to buy in the right areas and sell at the best times.

⇒ This is a long-term strategy that must be planned from the outset.

⇒ The risk is very low, as long as you meet your commitments.

⇒ The rental return is low initially and high at the end.

⇒ Capital growth is high initially and low at the end.

✦ ✦ ✦

In this chapter, we have looked at the various investment options that are available to you such as different types of properties and the opportunities they provide. The next step is the most crucial to the success of your investment. Of all the potential areas you have on your list, which is the suburb or town that is most likely to give you the growth or rental return that you want? The next chapter explores how to find the best investment areas, and shows you how to refine your search not just to where these suburbs and towns are, but according to when it is the right time to buy and to sell.

# Chapter 7

# How to find the best investment areas

The previous chapters have explored the property investment options available to you. They have outlined the vast differences between first-home buyers markets, rebuyer markets, and final seller and buyer markets. You should have a good idea of the type of areas and properties you want to invest in, such as high-growth areas, positively geared suburbs, houses or units, and in the city or the country.

This chapter will help you to find the best investment locations in each of these areas by providing you with cutting-edge techniques to locate areas with the best potential for capital growth or rental return. The techniques work for any area and will help to reduce your short list of suburbs to just a few that you can work with to find the types of properties you are looking for. In addition, these techniques show you the best time to sell your existing properties, so that you can achieve the maximum benefit from them.

They work best in combination — that is, you should not just use one method and ignore the others. It may be that there are unusual characteristics about the area that are skewing some of the statistics, and if they are the only statistics you are looking at, you will be misled. I will cover some of the problems associated with measuring the housing market and how important it is to understand the figures and assumptions behind them. Never trust any statistic unless you know how it was derived. If you can, use several sources to obtain the data you need.

You will learn how to interpret the data you obtain about the housing market in any area in terms of what renters, investors, buyers and sellers are thinking. Housing is about people and places, and people's ability to buy or rent them. If you can see what they are thinking and how they are acting in the areas you are interested in buying or selling, you can quite accurately judge whether prices or rents are about to increase or decrease, and which areas offer the best growth prospects. These techniques are designed to allow you to see what is going on in buyers', renters' and sellers' mindsets and understand their behaviour.

# Measuring the housing market

The main providers of housing information cannot seem to agree on what the value of housing really is. RPData, Residex, Australian Property Monitors, The Real Estate Institute of Australia and the Australian Bureau of Statistics will each give you a different median price for houses in Sydney or, indeed, for almost any housing data you are searching for. If they cannot agree on the basics, what hope is there for private investors who rely on the accuracy of their data to make crucial investment decisions? The answer is to understand what they are measuring and the methods they use to make the measurements. Measuring house prices and their movement is one of the most complex statistical processes there is. It is not at all like shares or commodities, where each unit is the same as any other, because every dwelling is different.

If you took the median value of the sales in one month and compared it with the median value of the sales the month before, you would be comparing completely different sets of sales. Not only would the properties be different, but the types of properties could also be different, leading you to make completely false assumptions about the change in housing prices. Let's assume that in one month mostly two-bedroom houses were sold, and in the next mostly three-bedroom houses were sold. The increase in median value from one month to the next could lead you to assume that a massive increase in prices had taken place. In fact, both the two- and three-bedroom houses may have fallen in value, and it was only the sale of more three-bedroom properties that caused the rise. Table 7.1 shows how deceptive the median price can be.

## Table 7.1: medians can be deceiving

| Year | Properties sold | Median price |
|------|-----------------|--------------|
| 1 | • 4 × two-bedroom houses sold for $200 000 each<br>• 5 × three-bedroom houses sold for $300 000 each<br>• 2 × four-bedroom houses sold for $450 000 each | $300 000 |
| 2 | • 6 × two-bedroom houses sold for $250 000 each<br>• 2 × three-bedroom houses sold for $350 000 each<br>• 2 × four-bedroom houses sold for $500 000 each | $250 000 |

Even though the price of houses sold in year 2 rose by \$50 000 each, the median price of all houses that were sold fell by \$50 000!

As you can see, investors cannot rely on the sales that are occurring now and compare them with the sales of a month, quarter or even a year ago to track price movements because each sale was for a different property. When a market is reacting to changes in demand or supply this can mean that the types of property in one quarter or one year can vary quite dramatically. Analysts who use the median price to measure these changes can be misled when this occurs because they are actually measuring the changes in the type of dwellings sold, rather than the actual change in price.

In 2008 to 2009 the price of houses appeared to fall and many experts called it that way. In fact, the opposite was happening, caused by the huge number of first-home buyers entering the market. This resulted in a drop in the median house price, due to the larger number of sales at the low end of the market. However, house prices were actually rising due to the increased demand, so even as the median house price fell, the price of houses was rising.

To get around this, analysts use different methods to more accurately calculate what the housing market is doing. These methods include measuring repeat sales or measuring the sale of properties with similar attributes such as bedrooms, bathrooms, garage spaces, land area, views and so on. Some merely provide the median sale price with all its shortcomings. The reason that each property analysis company or organisation arrives at a different result is because they are measuring different things. Not only that, but they can even differ on the area as well. Data providers must define what they mean by urban, city or suburban housing areas so that investors know which part of the market they are talking about.

Over time you would expect that all data providers would give the same results for large enough areas and, generally, they do, but it is important for you to know what the figures mean. If you are not sure, look at their methodology or ask them what the area being measured is, and what the data source is and the method used to provide the result.

Predicting the housing market is not an impossible task and by now you will have seen how the different markets in Australia react and respond to various changes in supply and demand. It is the job of property analysts to measure this reaction and its implications and they employ teams of highly qualified analysts, statisticians and researchers to monitor and identify these trends, and they are continually researching the market to identify changes in lifestyle and dwelling preferences. Yet they frequently seem to get it wrong. I have found that when historic housing data is overlaid with current demographic and economic trends, it is possible to make quite accurate forecasts about housing demand and prices. If, however, the wrong data is used, or it is incorrectly interpreted, quite ridiculous predictions can be made. For example, some analysts are predicting huge growth in the Adelaide property market, but table 7.2 shows that this is unlikely to be the case.

Table 7.2: Adelaide's property market, 2008 to 2010

| Year | Population growth | New households | Housing approvals | Surplus |
|------|-------------------|----------------|-------------------|---------|
| 2008 | 13720 | 5720 | 9811 | 4091 |
| 2009 | 15480 | 6450 | 8756 | 2306 |
| 2010 (est.) | 14600 | 6080 | 9955 | 3875 |

Source: Australian Demographic Statistics, Building Approvals, Australian Bureau of Statistics.

Based on Australian Bureau of Statistics figures of population growth, household size and building approvals in Adelaide, you may think that the city has a huge oversupply. Yet 90 per cent Adelaide's new households are created by overseas migrants. Adelaide also has a large interstate migration drain of young people heading to the eastern states in search of education, employment and lifestyle. What is happening is that the young people are leaving home and creating empty nests, while the migrant arrivals require immediate accommodation. The housing surplus is apparent but not real, at least not yet, but to predict any growth in such a market is risky.

You can unravel some of these mysteries of the market yourself by using demographic and housing data that is freely available from the Australian Bureau of Statistics website, and other sites such as the Real Estate Institute of Australia for local area data. There is a growing range of private websites that provide property data at suburb level for free. If you are particularly keen, you can even consult the National Library of Australia newspaper archives online and view every newspaper ever published in Australia right back to the earliest colonial days, as I did, to calculate rental history and house price movements — all you need is patience. A list of current sources of housing data is provided in the 'Further resources' section at the end of the book.

## Capital growth and rental return

Supply and demand are relatively constant at a national level, both increasing at about 2 per cent per annum, but as an investor, you are only concerned with the changes that occur at a local level. A new mining venture can cause sudden growth in demand and change the demographic make-up of households seeking accommodation, while its closure can have the opposite effect. A properly researched inner-city unit development can transform the appearance and attractiveness of the location and create demand from a new demographic.

In both examples, these will be either renters or owner-occupiers, and they will have an impact on the local market — resulting in either an increase in rent or capital growth. Nevertheless, over an extended period of time, almost all residential areas will produce the same average total return (rental return plus growth) as each other. This is because the natural interplay of supply and demand that causes people to move and dwellings to be built also reaches a point where the cost of rent or purchase is significantly greater than other similar or nearby areas and people move there instead. Housing returns gradually trend towards their long-term relative total return positions, regardless of whether they are cities, regions or suburbs. The only exceptions are towns where such movement is not possible — for example, mining towns, ports and resorts such as Port Hedland and Roxby Downs — where the captive demand ensures that high total returns can continue over long periods.

It is this long-term relationship between rents and prices that allows investors to determine which is likely to move next. For example, if recent capital growth has pushed prices up rapidly and caused rental returns to fall, it is likely that rents will increase more than prices in the near future, as it takes investors time to raise rents in response to the demand. This is because landlords cannot raise rents until tenants leave, or at the end of leases, so rents tend to lag behind capital growth in a high demand market.

One of the reasons Darwin has had high rental return (compared with other capital cities) and high capital growth in recent years is that the city has the highest interstate migration of any major city in Australia. About 20 per cent of the population arrive or leave each year, and this enables landlords to raise rents in response to demand far more easily and quickly than in other cities. While investors push up rents, it is prospective owner-occupiers who push up prices. When rents have risen rapidly in an area, the purchase of a property becomes comparatively more affordable and so potential owner-occupiers move into the buyer market, and prices rise.

You can measure the likelihood of either of these occurring by comparing the long-term capital growth and rental return performance of a suburb with its more recent performance. If the relationship between rent and prices (as measured by capital growth and rental return) is out of kilter, the one lagging behind is likely to catch up, especially if the recent annual average total return figure has been lower than the long-term annual average total return.

It is important to look at the dynamic of the local housing market to see whether there are market forces at work that may cause the current situation to continue, rather than correct. This also helps you estimate whether immediate growth or rent rises are possible — that is, have prices risen beyond those found in similar areas? Have rents recently escalated to their limits for such areas? It is also a good idea to look at the total sales over the last quarter compared with the last year. If the sales in the last quarter are more than a quarter of the year's sales, the area may be about to head into a growth phase, and if they are lower, rents are likely to rise.

You can analyse such suburbs more closely by using Google maps and street view to check that there is no obvious reason why sales, growth or rental returns have been low. It is also a good idea to look at recent listings and talk to local agents about the area. This will give you some anecdotal evidence to confirm or discount what the data is telling you.

**Rent versus growth checklist**

The following checklist will help you to assess the current state of an area:

⇒ Is the long-term (10-year) annual average total return higher than recent years?

- If yes, capital growth or rent increases are likely.
- If no, capital growth or rent increases are not likely.

⇒ Has the relationship between capital growth and rent return changed recently?

- If yes, the lower figure is about to rise.

⇒ Has the number of sales been falling or rising over the last year?

- If sales are rising, growth in prices is likely.
- If sales are falling, growth in rents is likely.

⇒ Are prices or rents at their upper limits compared with similar areas?

- If prices are high, rent increases are likely.
- If rents are high, price increases are likely.
- If both are high, neither prices nor rents are likely to rise.

Bear in mind that you need to treat mining towns differently when using long-term total return data, because periods of high growth can be quite lengthy, lasting more than 10 years. The search technique I have found to be highly accurate when comparing mining towns is to look for suburbs and towns with a long-term total return of more than 20 per cent per annum. They will most likely be mining towns, and you can then look at the rental return and capital growth in the previous year to see which way the town is heading. High growth and rent in the previous year indicates that the town should be investigated as potential for investment.

Do not be put off by the continued high growth — as long as the cause of growth remains, the growth will continue. When it reaches an unaffordable plateau, it simply translates into rent increases. For example, houses in Port Hedland, the richest mining town on the west coast of Western Australia, have reached a median value of more than $1 million. The rental return is only about 3 per cent, so it is highly likely that rents will go up rather than house prices, at least for the immediate future.

Rental return is a composite of rents and capital growth, which means that if rents remain static but prices fall, the rental return or yield goes up. Even if both fall, but prices tumble faster than rents, the rental yield will rise. So, using rental return to find positively geared properties is useless if the return is increasing because prices are falling. Investing in such areas is folly, yet many so-called positively geared lists contain such investment traps. Look at the actual rents — are they increasing or decreasing? Are capital growth and current rental return increasing or decreasing? Compare these with the long-term trends. You can then use this information to estimate which areas are overdue for a lift in prices or rent.

As you can see in table 7.3, a property bought in 2008 has lost 10 per cent in value, rent has fallen by 3.3 per cent and the actual rental return has dropped by 0.6 per cent, despite the apparent rise in return.

Information containing long-term capital growth, rental returns, sales and total returns is provided in many property investment magazines and in reports from data providers such as RP Data and Residex, which provide this data to the magazines. If you are seriously considering an investment, always check one data source against another if the result seems unbelievable, because it may be incorrect, and only checking will tell.

Table 7.3: apparent versus actual rental return

| Year | Median price | Weekly rent | Annual rent | Apparent return | Actual return |
|------|--------------|-------------|-------------|-----------------|---------------|
| 2008 | $300 000 | $300 | $15 600 | 5.2% | 5.2% |
| 2009 | $270 000 | $290 | $15 080 | 5.6% | 5.0% |

# The copycat effect

There is a phenomenon in the housing market known as the copycat effect. Put simply, it means that price rises in one area lead to rises in neighbouring areas. What happens is that the buyers move to more affordable areas and push up prices. This happens not just in suburbs where the type of housing is similar to housing in the area that has risen in price, but in neighbouring towns and even cities, as long as people have the desire to move. The reason for this is that we have a uniform system of housing finance, which means that right across the nation the ability to buy certain types of housing is the same for everyone. The lending rules and level of repayments are the same, so if one area rises in price, buyers move to a different area with similar housing types. It takes some time for people to realise that their dream home is now further away or in another part of the city than they thought it would be.

There are four large to mid-size cities in Tasmania, each within a few hours' drive of the other, and people move from one to the other as economic conditions and house prices dictate. Table 7.4 (overleaf) shows that there was a 15 per cent rise in the price of Hobart's houses during the first half of 2003, which was followed six months later by jumps in the median price in Launceston, Devonport and Burnie. Up to June 2004 the rate of annual growth in these cities was still higher than in Hobart. This happens every time the median house price rises significantly in Hobart, and while it may not happen next time, the example is useful to remember when looking at an area for investment, particularly in cities and larger towns.

## Table 7.4: the price ripple effect in Tasmanian cities

| City | Current median | Annual growth, June 2003 | Annual growth, December 2003 | Annual growth, June 2004 |
|------|----------------|--------------------------|------------------------------|--------------------------|
| Hobart | $374 000 | 39% | 15% | 8% |
| Launceston | $286 500 | 29% | 30% | 28% |
| Burnie | $275 000 | 28% | 40% | 25% |
| Devonport | $240 000 | 20% | 45% | 17% |

Source: Residex Quarterly Report for Tasmania.

Many developers ask me for historical price growth data to show their clients. 'Just look how much this area has grown in the last two years', their promotional material says. They offer this as proof that the area has good investment potential. However, the facts are quite the reverse — high growth rarely lasts longer than a few years and if it exceeds the long-term average, there is going to be a correction. Developers and their agents would be better served by informing their buyers of how much the surrounding towns have grown in value but their investment area has not. When you look at a locality or region, do not forget to look at its price relationship and growth history over the last three years compared with similar cities or localities. This simple exercise can quickly identify the areas that are about to grow and those that have just finished a growth spurt.

# Factors that drive house price growth

An expert may tell you that the Sydney market is about to boom or that Adelaide units are a good investment, but what use is this sort of information to you when you know that each type of house and each buying segment of the housing market behaves differently? This is why it is important to keep a close watch on the factors that drive certain types of housing growth. It is commonly accepted that first-home buyers will enter the market when interest rates are low and governments introduce schemes to encourage them. These may add to the motivation, but they are not the cause for buying.

The first cause is when rents start to approach the cost of repayments. At this point potential first-home buyers become motivated to buy a home of their own. Motivation can also come from a fall in interest rates. The early 1990s ushered in a period of rising rents, but this did not translate into first-home buying, because interest rates were also very high, coming off double-digit figures in the early part of the decade. Figure 7.1 shows that, due to the lack of first-home buyer activity, the housing market did not grow significantly in value in the 1990s.

Figure 7.1: the relationship between rents and house prices

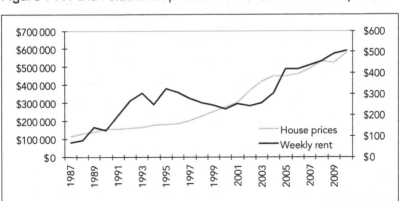

This brings us to the second cause for buying—confidence. Interest rates may be high, but first-home buyers seem to cope better with that than if rates are rising, even from a low base. Rising interest rates signify an attack on their household income and standard of living, and reduce their confidence in buying a home. Although interest rates fell significantly by the middle of the 1990s, they quickly rose again and potential homebuyers decided to remain renters. By the end of the decade a huge groundswell of disgruntled would-be buyers had built up, and interest rates had been low for some years. Confidence returned to buyers and first-home buyers entered the market in the thousands, sending the price of housing soaring. At the same time, rents remained where they had been for some years until a new generation of households started entering the rental market.

The third cause for buying is the lemming effect; that is, when one person does something, more people will follow suit. This can result in almost all renting households of the same generation trying to enter the homebuyer market at the same time, or in rebuyers of a certain generation upgrading at the same time. It also prompts potential retirees to sell their final home, or become investors at the same time. The mass movement sends prices up and ripples through the entire market, as we have seen.

When economists talk about interest rates and affordability, they do not consider the emotive part of the equation, yet what could be more emotive than buying a home? To judge the right time for first-home buyer activity in any market, watch the relationship between rents and repayments, and check whether interest rates have been steady or falling for at least a year. Any rise in rates or rents quickly bursts the confidence bubble.

At the other end of the market, a different set of economic circumstances motivates buyer activity and many of these are also investors. If you turn the factors that motivate first-home buyers on their head, you will be close to what motivates buyers at the high end of the market (that is, business owners and executives). Interest rates are far less important as investors can raise rents to compensate and the importance of rents is reversed, as the higher the rent the better the financing and gearing opportunities. Even high unemployment can motivate this market, for whom a pool of unemployed prospective employees is a good thing. A booming sharemarket lifts confidence and provides a source of deposit funds, while a booming economy drives up company profits. Again, it is the creation of confidence that is important. A shaky sharemarket will not do this, nor will a struggling economy. When there has been economic growth for some time the top end and the investor markets boom.

# High capital growth is short but sweet

Proponents of property investment will tell you that its growth is consistent and higher than any other form of investment. This is certainly true when you look at the long-term growth rate, which is more than 10 per cent per annum. However, what is also true about the housing market is that growth, when it occurs, can be very high and last only for a short time. You know that every housing market is different, why this is so and what to look for. Being aware of this characteristic of the market will see you escape the traps that so many investors fall into by believing that it does not matter where you invest, because the growth will occur anyway. We know that it will, but it could take a long time and investors are in a hurry. When you buy a property, you want to see immediate gains, not corrections or a stagnant market.

The short growth spurts and lengthy periods of little growth that occur can be seen at the macro level. Figure 7.2 (overleaf) shows the differences in growth in Sydney, Melbourne and Perth over a 10-year period.

## Figure 7.2: Sydney, Melbourne and Perth property markets, 2000 to 2010

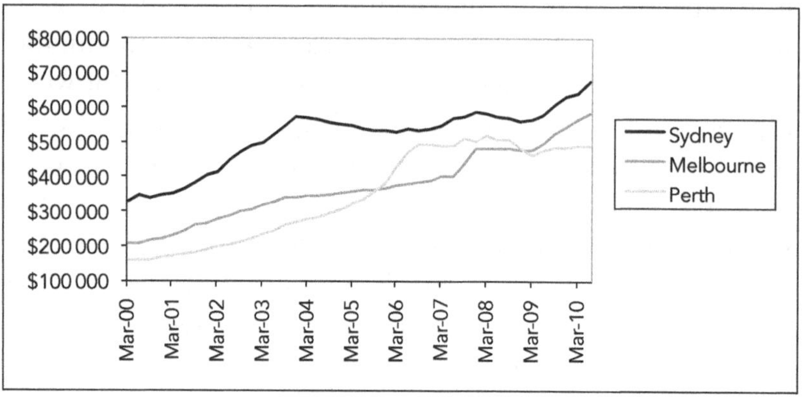

Source: Residex house price indices.

You can see the growth in the Sydney property market from 2002 to 2004, when house prices increased by more than $150 000, and you can also see what happened to the Sydney house market after the growth ended. It took five years for the median house value to reach its previous record of 2004, which is a long time to wait to get your money back.

The market in Perth had an even more spectacular rise, thanks to the minerals export boom. The graph shows Perth house prices increasing from $200 000 to nearly $500 000 in three short years. After two years of volatility and sleepless nights for investors, the inevitable crash came. Perth's house price growth over the 10-year period was almost 200 per cent, which indicates that the period of sleepless nights for investors who remain in that market is not over.

Melbourne's growth has been closest to the average of 10 per cent, and as a result it has not suffered any major corrections or falls in value. The rise in house value at the end of 2007 was about 20 per cent, but that was followed by a year of no growth, returning the market to its consistent average growth rate. Unfortunately, using the median in this way hides a great deal of what is actually going on in the city's micro market, but it does demonstrate the point.

What all this means to investors is that when you use the tools in this chapter to find areas that are about to grow, move in quickly and do not stay too long. Watch the signs that will tell you when it is time to sell and you will achieve far better results than those investors who hold and hope.

# Buyer mindsets determine medium-term growth

It is time to start thinking like a buyer. A common perception of buyers is that they are like a flock of seagulls fighting over a French-fry and only one will be successful. Nothing could be further from the truth, and understanding buyer behaviour can help you to pick boom areas before they occur and to avoid areas that are about to correct in value.

When buyers go shopping, price is one of the first points of difference they notice about similar products. The more expensive the product, the more important price becomes, and in the housing market it is usually the price — or, more accurately, their buying power — that limits what and where buyers can afford. This means that when prospective buyers are searching for properties, they look through newspapers and trawl listing websites, setting up watch lists and alerts in certain areas and for certain price ranges that suit their buying power.

This is an ongoing process and it results in growth for similar types of properties evening out over time. When prices rise in one area, buyers shift their search, not to the higher priced properties in that area, but to areas nearby, further along the train line or down the coast, where prices have not yet gone up. It means that areas with similar types of housing behave the same way over time and it is the constant movement of buyers that causes this, as shown in the growth predictions in table 7.5.

Table 7.5: buyer mindsets determine medium-term growth in similar suburbs

| Suburb | Median price | Long-term annual growth | 2007 | 2008 | 2009 | Growth prediction |
|--------|-------------|------------------------|------|------|------|-------------------|
| A | $325 000 | 12% | 16% | 13% | 8% | Low |
| B | $345 000 | 11% | 10% | 15% | 5% | Low |
| C | $324 000 | 10% | −2% | 8% | 5% | High |
| D | $356 000 | 8% | 0% | 12% | 5% | High |

When we look at the median prices of similar houses or units in demographically similar areas, however, there is still a large price variation. In some suburbs, prices may not have risen for a few years, while in similar nearby suburbs, prices may be shooting up. It may even be that prices are lower in the suburbs where there is no growth and higher in the suburbs that have experienced high recent growth. The reason for this is that while suburbs and towns may be similar, they are not the same. There will always be differences that result in each suburb or town having a median price that is different.

The key to unlocking this mystery is the relationship between long-term growth and short-term growth, and comparing the performance of areas you are interested in. This will tell you which areas have exceeded their long-term average in recent years and which areas are lagging behind. Comparing the long-term and recent performance of the areas you are interested in is an excellent indicator of buyer mindsets. Effectively, buyers in previous years have done the research for you and told you where and when they are about to start buying properties. While this does not allow you to predict absolute growth, it does give you an excellent indication of comparative growth — that is, which of the areas you have studied are likely to perform better than the rest in the next few years. This is because while each area will always have a different median house value, the long-term growth rate over 10 years will always tend to be achieved.

If we go forward further, we find that all long-term growth rates will trend to the long-term average for that city and, eventually, all long-term growth rates will trend to the Australian average. The trick is timing — that is, selecting the areas that are overdue for growth, not the areas that have just experienced high growth.

Comparing the performance of areas is not recommended for areas with consistently atypical growth, such as mining towns, ports and drought-affected areas. This method works well in larger cities, especially those with a substantially homogenous supply of similar types of houses, of the type you are interested in. Growth in four-bedroom houses may be very different from three-bedroom houses, when we looked at the different types of buyer markets and, for the same reasons, houses and units in the same area will perform very differently.

Many investors are misled into looking at suburbs that have achieved high growth in the last few years, in the belief that this will continue. Unless the conditions that caused the growth are set to continue, this is highly unlikely. In any case, it is likely that the demand will flow into rent increases rather than price rises. Understanding the buyer mindset saves you from falling into this trap and helps you to buy and sell at the best time. The data you need is the long-term and more recent annual growth figures with the median house or unit prices for a number of suburbs so that you can compare them. This information can be found in property investment magazines and in suburb reports, which can be purchased from the major data suppliers. Residex also produces a quarterly report with an annual supplement that provides annual growth figures for each suburb for the previous five years, which is an invaluable resource for this type of analysis.

## Seller mindsets determine short-term growth

We can also use the thinking processes of sellers to help us determine what the short-term growth potential for a suburb is. This information is particularly useful for investors seeking to flip or trade properties, and for renovators. Unlike buyers, who operate en masse as they move from one market to the other, vendors are like tigers, conducting a solitary search for that one elusive buyer. We can see what vendors are thinking by watching trends in listings, which are details of the property and their asking prices, and the median time that properties are listed on the market before they are sold. We can also follow their thought patterns by watching vendor discounting, which is the amount that the seller has reduced the asking price from its first listing to the amount it was sold for. These techniques are not possible with auctions, but enough properties are sold by private treaty to give us a good picture of what is going on.

In any market there is usually an even number of buyers and sellers over time, and the price of properties is the equaliser. Although there may be many potential buyers bidding for one property, these buyers will bid for many properties before they successfully buy one. If buyers outnumber sellers, then prices go up and the number of buyers reduces accordingly and more properties will come onto the market because of the higher prices. If sellers outnumber buyers, properties will stay on the market longer with the result that listings start to increase. Eventually, because of the low buyer interest, prices start to fall, sellers withdraw their properties from the market and others decide not to list their properties at all for the time being. This results in the number of listings falling and eventually prices start to rise again.

## Comparing listings with the median sale price

It may seem obvious, but how many investors would take the trouble to record the number of listings in the suburbs they are interested in over time? More importantly, how many would keep this sort of data in the areas in which they have investments? This data is very easy to find by trawling a major listing website and making a note of the total listings the same day each week. It does not matter if you do not get all the listings by using one listing site, because you will be taking a comprehensive sample. The way to use this data is to track the trend. There will be strange numbers appearing from time to time, but the trend will indicate what is going on. If you notice that listings are trending down over time, the price will probably go up, and if listings keep going up, the price is likely to go down.

Figure 7.3 (overleaf) shows how an increase in the number of listings is closely linked to falls in the sale price, and how a fall in the number of listings leads to an increase in price. It also shows that listings keep going up for a few months even after prices start falling, and that they fall for some time after prices are rising. This is because it takes time for the numbers to be made available and for buyers and sellers to react.

Figure 7.3: comparing listing count with median sale price

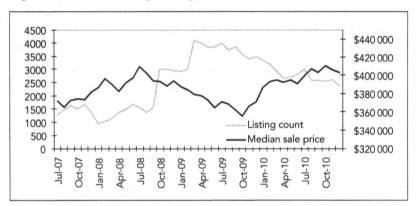

You now have a time window, a glimpse into the future, even if it is only a few months ahead. If you use this data with the following listing and sales techniques, you will have an eye into the future that few others have.

## Comparing vendor discounting with the median sale price

When owners with properties on the market want to sell in a market where sales are sluggish, they will be prompted by the estate agent to reduce the price or they may make this decision themselves. This is usually based on the few people turning up for open days and inspections, and lack of realistic offers. If this goes on for some time, it will have a negative effect on the market, both in terms of the current sale price dropping and what agents tell prospective vendors to expect for their properties. The effect of discounting, therefore, has an impact on prices many months into the future, as figure 7.4 shows.

## Figure 7.4: comparing vendor discounting with median sale price

When discounting starts to increase even as prices are rising, it signals the start of a price bust. For investors, this is a way of knowing when prices are going to fall up to many months ahead. It cannot tell you when prices are going to rise, as the rise in price precedes the fall in discounting. To measure discounting trends, you will need to record the initial asking price of new listings each week using a major listing website. Then check the local or metropolitan papers for the sales results when the property shows as sold in the listing site or disappears from the listing site, in which case it may also have been withdrawn from sale.

## Time on market trends

The longer a property is on the market, the greater the prospect of a reduction in price to secure a sale. Conversely, the shorter the time to sell, the greater the chance that prices will increase as this indicates good buyer demand. Figure 7.5 (overleaf) shows this effect with a consistent upward trend in time on market leading to a fall in prices in the future. As time on market reduces, prices start to pick up again.

Figure 7.5: comparing days on market with median sale price

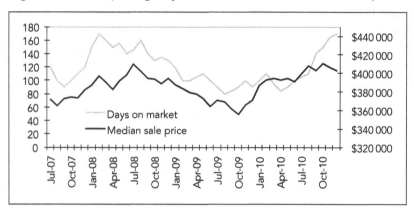

Understanding time on market trends is quite simple, and the trends act like an early warning signal:

➤ When time on market is *decreasing* and prices are *increasing*, a boom in prices is underway.

➤ When time on market is *increasing* and prices are *increasing*, a boom is about to end.

➤ When time on market is *increasing* and prices are *decreasing*, the property market is about to bust.

➤ When time on market is *decreasing* and prices are *decreasing*, the market is about to recover.

The lead time for the effects of time on market to flow into sellers' mindsets and cause them to change their asking prices means the effect in real time is almost the opposite of what you might expect: time on market is falling even while prices are falling and vice versa. This is an excellent way of tracking future price movements both ways, especially when used in conjunction with listing trends and discounting.

While time on market is available in property investment magazines and listing sites, the information is best collected from listing sites, as there are problems with the accuracy of the data from many published sources, which reduces the accuracy and value of the data. Keep track of when properties come on the market in the suburbs you are researching and when they are sold. Make a monthly list and take the middle figure, as this will show the trend more accurately than the average.

✦ ✦ ✦

These three data sets tell you what is going on in the mind of sellers. They allow you to get an insider's view into vendors' thinking that will lead to price reductions or price increases. With all these methods, the longer and more complete your data sets, the better the results will be. Ideally, it would be much more useful to track time on market, vendor discounting and listing trends just for the type of property you are looking to buy or sell, not for the entire housing market in the suburb. As a minimum, select either units or houses, and be sure to consult the newspapers, listing sites and sold data included in the 'Further resources' section at the end of this book on a weekly basis.

Be regular and systematic in building and maintaining a record of what vendors in your selected areas are up to. Remember, if the variation of types of houses is significant, the results may not be as accurate. Always use these analysis methods in conjunction with the other predictive methods included in this book as they are essentially for short-term estimation only.

## Watching the sales and listing trends

Earlier in this chapter, you saw how an increase in the number of sales in a housing market is usually a good sign of growth and a healthy buyer market. In its simplest form, this can be worked out by taking the annual number of sales and dividing by the number in the last quarter. If sales in the last quarter are more than 25 per cent of the total annual sales, then the market should be in a growth phase. This analysis of sales trends will also work for cities, even capital cities, as figure 7.6 shows.

Figure 7.6: measuring sales trends

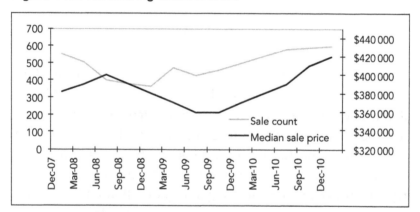

Looking at historical data it is possible to see how the market is behaving in terms of sales to prices and where the market is currently at. With access to the listing data as well as the sales data you can make some analytic assessments that can sometimes prove to be highly accurate. At the very least it gives you an insight into the local market that other investors are not aware of.

Understanding sales and listings trends is quite simple, and the trends act like an early warning signal:

➤ When sales are falling, listings are rising and prices are rising, the property market is about to correct.

➤ When sales are rising, listings are rising and prices are falling, the market is correcting.

➤ When sales are falling, listings are rising and prices are falling, the market is crashing.

➤ When sales are falling, listings are falling and prices are falling, the market is at the bottom of the crash.

➤ When sales are rising, listings are falling and prices are falling, the market is about to start recovering.

➤ When sales are rising, listings are rising and prices are rising, the market is in growth.

➤ When sales are rising, listings are falling and prices are rising, the market is booming.

➤ When sales are falling, listings are falling and prices are rising, the market is at the peak of the boom.

I would not recommend using the techniques outlined in this chapter in isolation, as they are not in themselves an accurate representation of market forces, but they can give you food for thought and perhaps lead you to the next boom.

# The importance of due diligence

I was inspecting some listings in a real estate agent's office and heard one salesperson say to another, 'At last, that one's off our hands'. Pity the poor buyer who was saddled with that property! Beyond all that statistics and data analysis can tell you, the final way to evaluate a suburb or town for growth potential is to have a look yourself. I have travelled to just about every town in Australia as part of my research into the property market and the first thing I do is drive down and then walk down the main street.

It's important to consider the following when conducting your own assessment:

➤ Are all the shops in business?

> ➤ Is there plenty of stock in the windows and are there customers inside?

> ➤ Do the restaurants and cafes appear to be doing good business?

Visit the local real estate agents and see how many listings and lettings they have, and the percentage that were recently sold or leased. Drive around the suburbs or the town and look at the state of the houses and gardens. If you cannot do this, ask a friend or relative to help out — due diligence requires that it must be done.

Things may not always be as they seem, as I discovered when researching a particular town. The website tourist guide had referred to the dam as a haven for water sports such as boating, sailing and fishing. It had seemed like the perfect destination for holidaymakers and retirees, and housing prices had actually fallen in recent years, promising excellent prospects for growth. However, when I rang the local real estate agent, I discovered that the town was on Level 5 water restrictions and the dam had been empty for over a year.

Use Google maps and street view to get an idea of what the area has to offer both locals and you as an investor. Do not rely on travel and tourist websites to tell you what an area is like because the information is likely to be out of date and biased. When buying remotely, the more you can find out, the less likely it will be that you have been wrong about the area and its potential.

✦ ✦ ✦

Armed with this wealth of tools and techniques, you can now select the best areas to meet your needs as an investor. This puts you at a distinct advantage, and you could purchase and sell properties and do quite well, but there is still one essential ingredient that is missing. Once you have selected a property, you need to know exactly how much it is worth. The reason is simple mathematics — the amount that you pay over the right price is profit for the vendor and the amount you sell under the correct price is profit for the buyer. Chapter 8 will help you to ensure that the profit in any transaction stays where it belongs — with you.

# Chapter 8

# Establishing the value of a property

One of the most important aspects of property investment is ensuring that you buy and sell at the best possible price. It is self-defeating to do the research, find the best areas and then throw it all away by paying way over the mark. In this chapter you will find out why almost every property price report, analysis, appraisal, valuation or estimate gives you a different result, and how to determine what the real worth of any residential property really is.

People make the decision to buy or sell a property based on all sorts of reasons. Owner-occupiers, for example, may pay over market value because they have fallen in love with the property, are sick of looking or because they have been misinformed. They may sell under market value because they are sick of waiting or need the money. Property seekers may buy for and sell for reasons other than price (such as appearance, location, features and ease of maintenance), but as an investor your head should always rule over your heart. If you have done the research and followed the steps in this book, you will be already looking in the right suburb, at the right time and at the right type of property, so your only point of comparison should now be the price you are prepared to pay.

A quick search online will show you that there is no need to be misinformed, with an array of free and paid property reports on offer. In addition, estate agents provide appraisals and comparative market analysis (CMA) reports for vendors, while virtually every property on the market will have had a valuation from a licensed valuer at some time in the past as these are often required by lenders before they provide buyers with finance.

All of these reports and services use the same data, which is a comparison of recent sales. Problems arise, however, because every report provided for any property is likely to give you a different value estimate. This is due to two reasons — the purpose of the report and the type of sales evidence that is being used to justify the estimate or price range provided. In some reports, no estimate is given at all, and you have to come to your own conclusions based on the information in the report.

# Why is it so hard to value residential property?

Unlike basic commodities or shares, where any unit sold is identical to every other, estimating property values is difficult because no two houses or units are the same. Even two identical houses in the same street will have different prices and two adjoining units in the same block will sell for different amounts because one has a better view than the other. To measure price change accurately over time you would have to set up a database recording and analysing all sales for the entire market. For this reason, most property price estimate reports take short cuts, which can give you an idea of a property's probable value. The most commonly used short cuts are as follows:

➤ *Median price.* This is the current median (or midpoint) price of houses or units in the immediate area or suburb of the property. The main limitation of using the median price is that the subject property may not be similar or typical of others in the area on which the median price is based.

➤ *Last sale price.* This is the last sale price of the property. The limitation of using this as an indicator of the property's current price is that the property may have increased in value since the last sale, and if the property has been improved the improvements will not be taken into account.

➤ *Upgraded last sale price.* This is the last sale price of the property upgraded to current prices using movement in the median price for the area. It should provide an accurate current worth estimate; however, if the property is at the high or low price end, the median price movement may not reflect the current price of the property. If the last sale was some years ago, price movements since then may make this estimate inaccurate. Also, if there have been improvements to the property since the last sale, they will not be taken into account.

➤ *Comparable sales.* This looks at recent sale prices of similar properties and estimates the price of the property based on these sales. While this is the best indicator to use, there are still significant problems. If there have been only a handful of recent sales, this means having to use non-comparable properties or properties located far away. The attributes (such as bedrooms, bathrooms, garage spaces, floor area and land area) may not be correct or even known. Another problem is that some attributes (such as views, aspect, development potential and distance to facilities) can sometimes be far more important in determining worth than other attributes. With units this is even more subjective, as unit values can vary dramatically depending on aspect and views.

You can see why each property estimate report and valuation is likely to provide you with a different result if they do not all use the same methods. Not only that, but the motives of the report providers themselves are also different and they will use the methods noted in ways that best meet their needs.

# Estate agent appraisals

Estate agents will usually provide prospective vendors with a free market appraisal of what the agent thinks the property will sell for in current market conditions. This is not a valuation or even a proper estimate. The estate agent's motives are different from the vendor's, who wants to obtain the highest possible price, or the buyer's, who wants the lowest possible price. The agent is concerned mainly with turnover, as the faster properties are sold, the greater their return by way of commission on sales.

The appraisal is designed to win the listing. It may contain some recent comparable sales or show similar properties listed on the market in the area and their asking prices — particularly those properties that the agent has listed or sold — but its primary purpose is to demonstrate how effective the agent is. The agent's appraisal is a marketing tool, designed to convince the buyer that the agent is best suited to win the listing. For this reason, an appraisal is of little use to potential buyers.

# Comparative market analysis reports from estate agents

Under state government law (which controls the buying and selling of land) estate agents must not make any false or misleading representations about a property, including any representations on price. Beyond the appraisal, they must provide a comparative market analysis (CMA) to show on what evidence their market opinion is based. While each state has different requirements for demonstrating this, the minimum requirement is usually for the agent to compare the appraisal with recent sale prices for at least three similar properties sold in the immediate vicinity.

An estate agent–provided CMA limits the extent to which agents can provide an incorrect appraisal about the worth of a property, but it is hardly an adequate tool for buyers. The sales evidence is easily manipulated by including only those recent sales that suit the agent's best interests and omitting those that do not. While I am not suggesting that agents would deliberately seek to mislead vendors, the system is nevertheless highly subjective. In effect, the CMA is used by the agent as part of, or in addition to, their appraisal and its whole purpose is to help the agent win the listing. For this reason, an estate agent–generated CMA is of little use to potential buyers and it is not in the agent's interest to disclose such information to buyers, as it might limit offers or bidding at auctions.

# Comparative market analysis reports from brokers

Mortgage brokers have started using the comparative market analysis (CMA) report as a lead-generation tool. Just as estate agents use CMA reports to win new listings, mortgage brokers use CMA reports to re-engage with old clients by showing them how much their property has increased in value, or to win new clients by offering a free CMA report showing them what their new property is really worth. They can also be an important part of brokers' promotional campaigns to secure new leads, convert leads to clients or develop relationships with clients. As a result, several property information companies have adapted their estate agent-designated CMA reports to suit brokers. Residex, for example, has developed a CMA report designed for brokers with marketing services targeted directly at new leads.

The key factors about these reports is that they are provided by an independent third party, they provide a wealth of information about the property and the housing market in the area, they supply local demographic information, and they are provided for free by the broker. These reports can be personally branded and include information from the broker for each specific situation.

## Physical valuations

Lenders may insist that buyers pay for a valuation from a licensed property valuer. The buyer does not get to choose the valuer — the valuer is selected from a list that the vendor uses, known as a valuer panel. The purpose of a valuation is to remove or reduce risk to the lender in providing the finance as regards the property's value, which is known to the lender as its 'security value'. There are other risks, such as the mortgagors' credit history or ability to repay, which are dealt with by the lender in other ways.

Lenders assess their security value risk in three ways:

> repossession history and likely repossession rates in the area where the property is located. This is important to the lender, as most mortgagee-in-possession sales occur within the first year or two of the life of a mortgage, and are far more prevalent in first-home buyer markets when

conditions such as interest rates and employment levels deteriorate

➤ the loan to value ratio (LVR), which is usually limited to 80 per cent or 90 per cent of the price being paid for it

➤ the amount of the loan.

If any of these present an unacceptable level of risk to the lender, a valuation is required. A valuation deals with risk to the lender in a couple of ways:

➤ it establishes a more accurate value of the property than the asking price — or, in the case of refinance, renovation or investment loans, a more accurate value of the property than the previous valuation, if there was one

➤ it protects the lender against possible loss, as the valuer must be personally insured against the subsequent losses that the lender may incur if the valuation proves to be inaccurate.

If the risk is still too high, the lender can insist that the borrower take out mortgage insurance to protect the lender if the borrower defaults and the property sells for less than the outstanding loan amount. In turn, mortgage insurers will normally insist that the property is valued.

If there is sufficient sales evidence to support the buyer's price, and the LVR is not too high, the valuer can drive past the property to ensure that it exists and is in good general condition. This is called a 'kerbside' or 'drive-by' valuation. A full physical valuation is usually only required when the LVR is over 80 per cent or the loan amount exceeds certain limits set by the lender.

The purpose of the valuation is to minimise risk, and this includes the valuer's risk. As a result, the valuer may be influenced by factors other than a comparison of recent sales and similar properties.

The condition of the property and state of the market in the area can lead the valuer to base their valuation on what is likely to happen, rather than on the current market situation. While this protects the lender, it does not protect the buyer, who usually pays current market value or more. A valuation, therefore, is not a good tool for buyers, as they can be expensive and buyers have to pay for them. In addition, it is ultimately a subjective analysis based on the valuer's experience and expertise, and the valuer's knowledge of the lender's needs.

# Electronic valuations

The development of sophisticated databases and analysis techniques has encouraged the gradual acceptance of electronic valuations (also known as automated valuation models or AVMs) by the lending community. AVMs use some or all of the property estimate tests mentioned earlier. They can also provide more than an estimate of a property's value, as they can show a value range within which the property's true value will lie and the probability of this estimate or range being correct. Not only are electronic valuations quicker and less expensive than physical valuations, they are completely objective.

There are four reasons why AVMs have only gradually been adopted by the lending community, and even then only in low-risk situations:

➤ The finance sector is by nature conservative and unwilling to go out on a limb. When it does, the motive is usually profit, and as the borrowers pay the cost of valuations there is little benefit to the lender except the time saving.

➤ One of the main benefits of a physical valuation is that it proves to the lender that the property actually exists, as claimed by the borrower. The valuer can also certify to the condition of the property and the value of any improvements made since the last sale. The valuer can also select recently sold properties by their physical match to the subject property, rather than by an electronic matching of attributes that may or may not be up to date.

> The existing valuation industry sees AVMs as an amorphous competitor, which if adopted by lenders could have a negative impact on their livelihood. Rather than accept the AVM as a tool that they can derive commercial benefit from, their tactics have been to lobby lenders against the use of AVMs.

> The subprime mortgage crisis and subsequent house price falls damaged the credibility of AVMs in the US and UK, which had been providing house prices based on a continuation of the status quo. While there is no evidence that sworn valuers would have given different valuations, it was the AVM market that took the brunt of the fallout and severely dented their reputation.

Nevertheless, lenders are increasingly relying on AVMs where the LVR is so low that that there is virtually no risk to the lender. This is because they can be processed quickly and inexpensively. While AVMs are not available to investors as a property price estimation tool, they use the same techniques provided in paid property price estimate reports.

# Free property price estimates and reports

There is a plethora of free property price estimate reports, or services claiming to provide such reports in the market, available from websites such as What Price My House, MyHouseValue, OzHomeValue and HomeGuru. These usually provide basic demographic information and housing market history of the suburb or postcode, and some also provide a list of recent sales in the area and the median value of homes in the area. In some cases the basic suburb information is included with a note that a local estate agent will be in touch to provide their market appraisal.

These are almost always tools to gather information that can be sold or passed on to estate agents, mortgage brokers or other interested parties. This is clear from the level of questioning that some of the providers insist on — it goes way beyond what would be required to provide a property report. The reports that are sent often prove to be completely inadequate for accurate property pricing, and can result in a succession of telephone calls and emails from people to whom the contact details have been passed on, in order to sell other services to the unsuspecting enquirer.

I recommend instead using the basic housing price information available for free from RP Data <www.myrp.com.au> (which also provides mapping and recent sales information), Australian Property Monitors <www.homepriceguide.com.au> (which also provides sales history in the area), and Residex <www.find meahome.com.au> and <www.residex.com.au> (which gives free price estimates).

## Property price estimates and reports you pay for

The main property information companies such as RP Data, Australian Property Monitors and Residex also sell individual property price reports online. They vary in price and quality, but will provide local demographic information, a history of sales and prices in the area, and a list of recent comparable sales. Some will also provide a price estimate or price range for the property, or explain how to estimate it yourself, and include a forecast for the next year's growth or next five and eight years' growth.

These reports include FindMeAHome's 'Right Price' report, Residex's 'Property Explorer' report, Home Price Guide's 'Property Report', and RP Data's 'Individual Property Report' (with no property price estimate) and 'RP Estimate Report'. Prices range from about $50 to $75 each, and specials and other discount offers are periodically offered. Each of these companies also offers a wide range of street, suburb and postcode housing market reports online.

## Other features to consider

It is crucial for potential buyers, especially investors, to be aware of the correct price for a property on the market, and never offer or bid more than it is worth. The best means of determining the correct price is by buying one or more of the paid property reports discussed earlier in the chapter, and using the information to come to your own conclusion regarding the price. If, however you are using a mortgage broker, chances are they will provide you with a free CMA report that contains all the information you will need.

I would not recommend valuing the property yourself, but if you are quite keen to do so the correct technique is to do what a valuer does. Compare the property and its attributes (such as bedrooms, bathrooms, garage spaces, aspect, land size, floor area, views, proximity to services and condition) to recently sold properties of comparable attributes in the immediate area. Then make an estimate of the property's value by comparing it with the sale price of the other properties.

There are many other features you need to consider when assessing the value of a property or its suitability as an investment. You need to be sure about the likely level of renter demand for you property:

➤ What sorts of tenants are attracted to the suburb and what motivates them to live there?

> ➤ Will prospective tenants be attracted to your property?

> ➤ Is the property located close to the services that will be required by prospective tenants?

> ➤ Are the type, size and style of the property in demand by renters in the area?

It is also important to check with local authorities about possible developments that may affect the value of your property or its ability to be rented out in the future, such as air traffic corridors, freeway extensions or other infrastructure developments planned for the area. Look for zoning plans and the council's urban development plan for the area — its website is a good place to do this. Also check heritage listings to make sure your property or street is not encumbered in some way.

If you are searching in summer, make sure the land is not flood-prone in winter, and if you are looking in the cooler months, check that the land is not in an area subject to threats from bushfires. Check the local water supply and whether there are any water restrictions. Finally, if you are in the area, check out the condition of the neighbouring properties. They (or the neighbours themselves) may detract from the appeal of your property.

✦ ✦ ✦

The next chapter provides a simple plan you can use, as well as case studies, to make sure that you have covered everything when embarking on your investment journey.

# Chapter 9

# Your property investment plan

It has been said that if you fail to plan, you plan to fail. This is certainly so in the property investment market—not only is it an extremely complex investment option, it also involves greater amounts of capital than other investments. The cost of failure is simply too high, yet investors do fail, or at least they fail to make the most of the opportunities that the residential property market offers them.

Planning to be successful involves making the right decisions about buying and selling property, and this in turn requires a dedicated approach to the housing market. The sharemarket allows investors to look up the value of their holdings at any time, and the company determines both the amount of the dividend and its payment to the investor. To know the value of your properties at any time is not so easy, and knowing when to sell is even more complex. You are also in control of the rental dividend, at least to the point that if you do not charge enough, your tenants will not tell you and if you charge too much they will simply choose to rent elsewhere and your properties will be harder to let. You need to monitor the progress of your investments at all times, not just to know when to sell, but to know how much rent to charge.

There are many books on the market that will explain how to negotiate a good price when buying, manage your finances and balance your investments, and flip, trade, renovate or buy properties for development. This book, however, deals with the most important aspects of property investment — when and where to buy and when to sell to get the best returns. I am dismayed when I hear stories told by some advisers and investors who state that they bought in a certain suburb or town because they had a 'gut feel' about it or 'it looked like a good area to invest in'. This is not a sensible way to approach such a significant undertaking. A structured approach to housing investment is essential and the plan in this chapter shows you how to use the tools and techniques I have explained to get the best possible results from housing.

If you are seeking good capital growth, there is little point buying a property in an area that has just seen significant growth, as you will end up waiting for years while prices stagnate. Neither does it make sense to buy a positively geared investment in an area that is oversupplied with investment properties, as this will lead to the financial pain of lengthy vacancy rates and falling rents as investors compete for tenants. These are common enough experiences yet they are easy to avoid. By following my plan, you will minimise the chances of these things happening to you, and maximise your opportunities for successful investing.

To demonstrate how this plan and the techniques in this book can best be used, I have also included three different case studies. It should be noted that the suburb data I have used and the conclusions drawn from it are only for the purposes of these case studies. Although the analysis techniques are valid any time they are used, they will produce different results in the future because the relative investment merits of each suburb and town change over time.

# Planning your investment journey

It is essential to create a housing investment plan that will work for you. Having a plan will help you to select areas and buy properties most suited to meeting your goals. It will also help you to monitor and reassess the performance of your investments at all times to make sure your goals are being met.

## Investment goals

Before starting your investment journey, determine exactly what you want to achieve and how you will start. Establish how much capital you have and how much you can borrow. Work out what your goals are — for example:

➤ Start a property investment portfolio.

➤ Achieve high capital growth and increase my portfolio.

➤ Achieve a high enough return to maintain my lifestyle.

Make sure you write your goals down so you can refer back to them whenever you feel like you are losing your way.

## Expected results

Once you have established what your goals are, the next step is to work out how you will achieve them. Should you opt for:

> maximum growth in the shortest time?

> investments that pay for themselves?

> high capital growth with low risk?

> renovating, flipping or trading?

> high rental returns with low risk?

## Housing investment options

Now it is time to assess what your property investment options are. You will need to work out where you can afford to buy, and then consider whether to:

> buy houses or units

> invest in the city or the country

> detonate, renovate or wait

> buy an existing property or purchase off the plan.

## Optimum areas and property types

By this stage you should have a good idea of which areas to search in. The next step is to put together a short list of the areas with the most potential (I would recommend using a spreadsheet for this). The list should include the following details:

> price range (for example, $250 000 to $300 000)

> property type (for example, low maintenance units)

- ➤ market (for example, Sydney or Melbourne)

- ➤ area (for example, middle-distance older suburbs)

- ➤ strategy (for example, buy and hold for four years)

- ➤ goal (for example, high short-term growth)

- ➤ rental yield (for example, minimum 6 per cent).

## Market analysis of selected areas

Using the tools and techniques in chapter 7 (such as rent versus growth, long-term and short-term growth, and sales and listings trends), reduce your short list to the best one or two suburbs.

## Selected properties

Make a list of the properties on the market in the suburbs you have chosen and find out their true worth. You can do this by either purchasing a property price estimate report from a reputable property information provider or by conducting your own analysis of recent sale prices of comparable properties in the immediate area, as shown in chapter 8. Make offers based on these values, and do not go over them.

## Your progress

Maintain a spreadsheet showing the progress of your investments, with current estimated values and current rental return, as shown in table 9.1 (overleaf). Use the tools and techniques described in chapter 7 to maintain a regular health check on each investment.

Table 9.1: sample progress spreadsheet

| Address | Date bought | Price paid | Current rent | Current yield | Current estimate | Total growth | Analysis |
|---|---|---|---|---|---|---|---|
| 4 South St | Mar 05 | $260 000 | $320 | 6.4% | $530 000 | 104% | Hold |
| 1 East St | May 07 | $300 000 | $400 | 6.9% | $550 000 | 83% | Sell |
| 2 West Rd | Jun 09 | $320 000 | $340 | 5.5% | $360 000 | 12.5% | Hold |

By keeping an eye on your investments you will know not just which property you should sell next, but when the best time is to sell.

# Case study 1: first-time investor, Graham

Graham is 31 years of age. He is currently renting with friends and wants start investing in housing. His buying power is $300 000 — taking into account savings of $30 000 and allowing $10 000 for purchasing costs, stamp duty and a contingency account to cover unexpected costs and periods when there is no rent coming in.

## Investment goals

Graham's aim is to build a portfolio of four or five investment properties within 10 years and eventually live off the income from his investments.

## Expected results and investment options

Graham has decided that his first investment must achieve rapid growth in the shortest possible time and that he should therefore invest in a mining town.

## Optimum areas and property types

Based on his research, Graham decides that, in the immediate future, east coast coal is less risky than west coast iron ore or South Australian mining towns, and settles on Queensland coalmining towns. Using the options presented in chapter 6 he opts to buy a house rather than a unit, and plans to hold the property for at least two years. He chooses a near-new property to minimise maintenance costs, which will still give him substantial depreciation benefits.

## Market analysis of selected areas

Graham's purchase price range is up to $300 000 and he uses the tools and techniques explained in chapter 7 to reduce the possible areas to the three best for his first investment property. His preliminary short list includes locations with the following attributes:

➤ long-term average annual total return of at least 20 per cent per annum

➤ towns with at least 10 sales in the previous quarter

➤ towns with high rental yields

➤ towns where growth in the last year has been maintained.

He obtains this data from property investment magazines and uses the Residex quarterly report for Queensland, which provides all the information he needs. He makes up a list of all towns and suburbs in Queensland with total returns more than 20 per cent average per annum, omitting those with extremely low sales during the last year or quarter, as these are obviously not going to be good areas to buy into.

While this will not show Graham mining towns that have recently been developed, it is a good strategy for locating existing and expanding coalmining towns in the Bowen and Surat basins. Mining has been carried out in some of these areas for generations and the locations of the major coal seams are fairly well known. Graham's initial list, ranked in order of current median house values, is shown in table 9.2.

Table 9.2: initial mining town short list

| Town | Total annual average return (10 years) | Last year's growth | Rental yield | Rental yield trend | Sales in last quarter | Median value |
|---|---|---|---|---|---|---|
| Dysart | 32% | 21% | 6.0% | Falling | 8 | $447 500 |
| Moranbah | 32% | 7% | 6.6% | Falling | 50 | $446 000 |
| Berrinba | 35% | 15% | 4.9% | Falling | 1 | $410 500 |
| Clermont | 24% | 11% | 5.5% | Falling | 11 | $299 500 |
| Blackwater | 26% | 1% | 5.8% | Falling | 44 | $279 500 |
| Miles | 22% | 5% | 6.1% | Falling | 10 | $237 000 |
| Glenwood | 23% | 1% | 5.6% | Falling | 10 | $226 500 |
| Wandoan | 20% | 15% | 6.6% | Steady | 8 | $207 500 |
| Collinsville | 27% | 12% | 7.6% | Falling | 10 | $201 000 |
| Surat | 25% | 9% | 7.8% | Falling | 2 | $163 000 |
| Mt Morgan | 24% | 6% | 6.0% | Falling | 17 | $150 000 |

While Dysart is his first choice based on the continuing high capital growth rate and good rental yield, its median value is too high and sales are too low. He checks listing websites and discovers that the listed properties are all out of his buying reach. Moranbah is also too expensive, and growth is falling. This latter factor also excludes Blackwater, Miles, Glenwood and Mount Morgan.

After undertaking further research, he discovers that although Clermont has had high long-term and recent growth, it is not a mining town and should not be in his list. Berrinba has too few sales and is also excluded. Table 9.3 shows Graham's revised short list, which now includes just three towns.

Table 9.3: final mining town short list

| Town | Total annual average return (10 years) | Last year's growth | Rental yield | Rental yield trend | Sales in last quarter | Median value |
|------|------|------|------|------|------|------|
| Wandoan | 20% | 15% | 6.6% | Steady | 8 | $207 500 |
| Collinsville | 27% | 12% | 7.6% | Falling | 10 | $201 000 |
| Surat | 25% | 9% | 7.8% | Falling | 2 | $163 000 |

Graham's next task is to consult the listing data he has collected on these towns from researching listing websites and property investment magazines. He compares the listings, sales, time on market, and recent prices and rents data, as shown in table 9.4 (overleaf).

In Wandoan and Collinsville, the falling time on market trend and rising prices suggest that a boom is underway. In Surat, rising time on market with sluggish price growth indicates that a boom is about to end. The sales and listings trends support these findings in each town. This suggests that Surat's housing market, with falling sales, listings and steady prices, is at the end of a boom following a long period of high growth. Even mining towns have their downturns.

## Table 9.4: sales and listings data

| Town | Sales trend | Listings trend | Time on market trend | Prices in last quarter | Rents in last quarter |
|------|-------------|----------------|----------------------|------------------------|-----------------------|
| Wandoan | Rising strongly | Rising | Falling | Rising | Steady |
| Collinsville | Rising strongly | Falling | Falling | Rising | Rising |
| Surat | Falling | Falling | Rising | Steady | Steady |

Wandoan and Collinsville present as towns about to enter strong growth phases, with sales rising strongly (50 per cent of the annual sales occurring in the last three months), rising listing trends and rising prices. Despite this obvious potential for growth, the rents in Collinsville are also rising strongly. When Graham investigates this, he finds that houses can be purchased for about $170 000 and attract rent of up to $300 per week. He realises that he can afford two three-bedroom houses in Collinsville at his purchasing power limit and decides to pursue this goal. This will not only give him potential for good capital growth, but a higher rental return than if he purchased one house at a higher price.

## Property selection process

Graham has about 100 properties to choose from in Collinsville, but he cannot check them out in person. By looking at the listings, types of houses and asking prices, he has a good idea of the local market. He checks the streets using Google street view, checks local websites and talks to local agents on the phone to get a good idea of the conditions and rentability of each property. He knows the importance of getting an independent property price report and not relying on any anecdotal evidence. He realises it is better not to buy than to pay too much, and the greater the selling pressure the more desperate the salesperson must be. Within a few weeks he has chosen two properties to buy.

## Monitoring process

Although Graham's aim was to increase his equity as quickly as possible, he has managed to buy two properties for less than $160 000 each and been able to rent out each for more than $250 per week. He can look forward to seeing these properties become positively geared very quickly. Yet because his aim is to secure high growth, he needs to maintain some basic data records about sales and vendor listing trends. These will let him know if the growth is likely to continue or if it is about to end and he should sell his properties. He can do this by simply maintaining the database he set up at the start of his search process.

What he needs to watch are increases in vendor discounting and time on market trends, as these will give advance warning of an imminent fall in prices even while prices are still rising. He needs to keep an eye an the sales and listings checklist. When he purchased, the number of sales and sale prices were increasing, while the number of listings was falling, indicating a market in growth. If the sales trend starts to slow, even while the other trends do not change, this indicates that the market has peaked. By the time that listings start to rise, Graham will have sold his properties before prices start to correct.

To secure the best result, Graham should sell his properties in Collinsville when the following conditions occur:

> prices are still increasing, but sales and listings are trending down

> prices are still increasing, but so is time on market

> prices are still increasing, but so is the amount of vendor discounting.

Graham will have left it too late if he tries to sell when prices are still rising, but sales are trending down and listings are trending up.

# Case study 2: badly advised investor, Shukla

Shukla is aged 42, self-employed and has been happily divorced for several years. Unfortunately, she was given some unsound investment advice after her divorce settlement, which has placed her in a position where she cannot make any further investments without selling one of her two investment properties (both in Victoria), and she is unsure of her best options.

## Investment goals

Shukla has an investment property in Ringwood, which is an off-the-plan unit she bought after her settlement. It is now generating sufficient rent to cover the repayments. Shukla also has a house in Geelong, which she bought in 2009 and which is negatively geared. Shukla borrowed heavily against the equity in her home to set up her business and buy the house in Geelong, and she has no further borrowing power. She cannot invest further without selling one of her properties, but she is unsure whether to do this, and if so, which one to sell. If Shukla decides to sell one property, she then needs to determine what type of investment property is best suited to her needs and where to buy it to get the best results.

## Current portfolio and investment options

Shukla obtains comparative market analysis reports from her mortgage broker to show her the current value of each of her properties. This shows her the growth each property has achieved and the current rental yield she is obtaining. The performance of Shukla's investments is shown in table 9.5.

Table 9.5: property portfolio performance

| Suburb | Year bought | Price paid | Current value | Current rent | Rental yield | Annual growth |
|--------|-------------|------------|---------------|--------------|--------------|---------------|
| Ringwood (unit) | 2007 | $380 000 | $428 000 | $370 | 5.1% | 5% |
| Geelong (house) | 2009 | $410 000 | $441 000 | $380 | 4.8% | 4% |

Shukla uses the techniques explained in chapter 7 to compare the current and potential performance of each investment area for the type of property she owns. This can be seen in table 9.6 (overleaf).

## Table 9.6: potential capital growth performance

| Suburb | Long-term average annual growth | Growth three years ago | Growth two years ago | Growth last year | Estimated future growth |
|---|---|---|---|---|---|
| Ringwood (unit) | 11% | 2% | 10% | 21% | Low |
| Geelong (house) | 10% | 2% | 9% | 7% | High |

According to the data, Ringwood units have experienced a boom in prices over the last two years, yet her unit has only grown in value by 5 per cent per year. This suggests that she paid far too much for the property and the recent high growth compared with the long-term average suggests that the growth is unlikely to continue. Her house in Geelong has grown in value by 4 per cent during the last year, while the median value rose by 7 per cent, indicating that she also paid more than market value for that property, although not to such a great extent. She can see that growth in Geelong is low compared with the long-term growth average, and it is much lower than similar nearby areas such as Geelong West where the previous year's growth was almost double. This means there is every chance that the value of her house will rise substantially in the near future.

Shukla weighs up the potential for rent or capital growth to help her decide which property to put on the market, as shown in table 9.7.

Table 9.7: relative potential for rent or capital growth

| Suburb | Long-term total return | Recent total return | Which return is higher? | Capital growth and rental return | Sales trend: falling or rising | Rents compared with nearby areas |
|---|---|---|---|---|---|---|
| Ringwood (unit) | 17% | 26% | Recent | Yield falling | Steady | Lower |
| Geelong (house) | 15% | 12% | Long term | Yield steady | Rising | Higher |

Shukla can see that the long-term total return for Ringwood units is less than the recent total return, indicating that the prospect for rent rises or growth is less likely than in Geelong, where the long-term total return is higher than the previous year. The relationship between capital growth and rental return has changed in Ringwood, with the falling yield indicating that rents are more likely to rise than prices. The trend in house sales is rising in Geelong, indicating that growth is on the way, but is steady in the Ringwood unit market.

When Shukla compares rents with nearby similar areas she discovers that Ringwood rents are lower, while in Geelong they are higher. This indicates that prices are more likely to rise in Geelong. Each of the tests, plus the other data she has obtained, indicate that Geelong is a definite hold property and Ringwood is the one to sell. Unfortunately for Shukla, the data also clearly showed that she paid too much for the Ringwood unit and, as a result, missed out on the price boom that occurred.

# Due diligence

Having made her decision based on logical research, Shukla sells the Ringwood unit for $430 000. She then undertakes due diligence for the property in Geelong to ensure she does not get caught out if the market starts to soften. Shukla puts together a watch list to record Geelong's house listings, sales, time on market and vendor discounting trends, so she can be sure to sell her house at the best time, as shown in table 9.8.

Table 9.8: sales, listings, time on market and vendor discount watch list

| Week | Sales | Listings | Time on market | Vendor discounting | Median sale price |
|------|-------|----------|----------------|--------------------|-------------------|
| 1 | 3 | 45 | 60 days | 5% | $490 000 |
| 2 | 4 | 50 | 80 days | 4% | $470 000 |
| 3 | 2 | 43 | 70 days | 5% | $430 000 |
| 4 | 1 | 60 | 70 days | 6% | $500 000 |
| 5 | 2 | 65 | 80 days | 7% | $510 000 |
| 6 | | | | | |
| 7 | | | | | |
| 8 | | | | | |

Shukla keeps a record of new listings each week from one major listing website. She follows the properties until they appear in the sold section of her newspaper. Then she knows their time on market and the discounting that occurred. She also checks her results periodically against those provided in property investment magazines each month. By maintaining a watch list and reading the trends and their meanings, Shukla will never get caught buying or selling at the wrong time.

## Market analysis of selected areas

Shukla is determined not to get burnt again. She decides high capital growth with low risk is her only option, so that she can use the equity to build her portfolio. She does not want the risks associated with mining towns, and decides that she will invest in one of the major regional centres along the Murray River that is recovering from the drought. She hopes to gain from the increase in industry, employment and housing demand that will follow.

Shukla uses the methods outlined in chapter 7, such as following the ripple effect and thinking like a buyer, to determine which areas are about to grow before the others (her initial short list is shown in table 9.9, overleaf). She realises that because of the drought, the long-term average annual growth rate will be much lower than most other areas and also lower than the national average, but she also knows that this means the short-term growth rate is likely to be much higher as a result, now that normal conditions have returned to this market. This allows her to come up with some conditions to find the best town to invest in:

➤ the long-term average should be higher than recent years, but with some growth starting

➤ towns with at least 10 sales in the last quarter

➤ towns with median values of not more than $210 000, so that she can buy two properties.

## Table 9.9: initial Murray River towns short list

| Town | Long-term average annual growth | Growth three years ago | Growth two years ago | Growth last year | Sales in last quarter | Sales trend | Median value |
|------|------|------|------|------|------|------|------|
| Renmark | 8% | 2% | 4% | 6% | 24 | Rising | $187 500 |
| Berri | 7% | 3% | 5% | 6% | 18 | Rising | $192 000 |
| Barmera | 6% | –2% | –5% | –4% | 10 | Falling | $170 000 |
| Loxton | 7% | 2% | –3% | –2% | 24 | Rising | $195 000 |
| Cobram | 7% | –2% | 1% | 2% | 27 | Steady | $210 000 |
| Mooroopna | 8% | –2% | 0% | 7% | 35 | Rising | $210 000 |
| Rochester | 7% | 1% | 2% | 4% | 17 | Steady | $197 000 |
| Mildura | 6% | 4% | 2% | 1% | 194 | Rising | $210 000 |

Shukla can see that growth has already started, although from a very low base, in some of the initially selected towns. It is likely that by the time she finds a property in Mooroopna, Renmark or Berri it may be too late to catch the initial growth surge. This does not concern her, because there are other towns where growth is yet to occur and sales have not started trending upwards. On the other hand, the conditions in Barmera and Loxton could be so severe that it may take more than just high rainfall and water flowing down the Murray to restore the economic fortunes of such towns. The final short list she arrives at is shown in table 9.10.

## Table 9.10: final Murray River towns short list

| Town | Long-term average annual growth | Growth three years ago | Growth two years ago | Growth last year | Sales in last quarter | Sales trend | Median value |
|------|------|------|------|------|------|------|------|
| Cobram | 7% | –2% | 1% | 2% | 27 | Steady | $210000 |
| Mildura | 6% | 4% | 2% | 1% | 194 | Rising | $210000 |

Shukla purchases a house in Cobram and another in Mildura using the tools in chapter 8 to make sure that she pays the right price for each. She then maintains a watch list for each town to make sure that she sells at the right time, as shown in table 9.11.

## Table 9.11: sales, listings, time on market and vendor discount watch list for Cobram

| Week | Sales | Listings | Time on market | Vendor discounting | Median sale price |
|------|-------|----------|----------------|--------------------|--------------------|
| 1 | 2 | 40 | 75 days | 5% | $210000 |
| 2 | 1 | 45 | 60 days | 4% | $210000 |
| 3 | 3 | 43 | 70 days | 5% | $215000 |
| 4 | 4 | 38 | 70 days | 6% | $214000 |
| 5 | 4 | 35 | 60 days | 7% | $217000 |
| 6 | | | | | |
| 7 | | | | | |
| 8 | | | | | |

Over the next months, Shukla maintains her watch lists for Cobram and Mildura, as well as for Geelong. She sets up property alerts with the major property listing websites so that she knows when properties have come onto the market, and notes their initial asking price. She keeps an eye on the sold columns in the local newspapers to find out when the properties were sold, and so she knows how long they were on the market for and what the discount was for each property. Shukla also establishes a weekly routine of due diligence, so that she will know exactly when to put each property on the market to get the best possible price.

By doing so, Shukla will be ready when the figures tell her it is time to sell. At the same time, she continues researching other areas for investment opportunities. This will help Shukla achieve a far higher return with each successive investment than those investors who rely on gut feel or what they read in the press. Within a few years, she will be well on the way to achieving her goals.

# Case study 3: Harry and Jen at the turning point

Harry and Jen are approaching retirement and have four investment properties in New South Wales — two off-the-plan units in Penrith, a house in Armidale and a house in Dalmeny. They borrowed 90 per cent of the price of the units and still owe most of the purchase price of the Dalmeny property, as it has not grown in value anywhere near what they expected when they first fell in love with it. They want to start converting their investments into high-rental producing properties, but although the rents from their four properties are meeting the interest repayments, they cannot borrow more.

# Current portfolio and investment options

Harry and Jen buy some property price investment reports to evaluate the current state of their portfolio and determine their best strategy. The performance of their properties is shown in table 9.12.

Table 9.12: property portfolio performance

| Suburb | Year bought | Price paid | Current value | Current rent | Rental yield | Annual growth |
|---|---|---|---|---|---|---|
| Dalmeny (house) | 2007 | $290000 | $326000 | $300 | 5.4% | 4% |
| Armidale (house) | 2009 | $300000 | $327000 | $305 | 5.3% | 9% |
| Penrith (unit) | 2010 | $276000 | $270500 | $270 | 5.0% | –2% |
| Penrith (unit) | 2010 | $276000 | $270500 | $270 | 5.0% | –2% |

Then they use the techniques explained in chapter 7 to compare the potential capital growth performance of each investment area for the type of property they own, as shown in table 9.13 (overleaf).

Comparing the potential capital growth performance shows Harry and Jen that the house in Dalmeny has the highest future growth potential, while the recently purchased units have the lowest and were not a good growth investment. The question they need answered now is which of these investments will provide the best rent returns. They use the rent or growth rule to help them decide which property to put on the market, as shown in table 9.14 (on page 201).

Table 9.13: potential capital growth performance

| Suburb | Long-term average annual growth | Growth three years ago | Growth two years ago | Growth last year | Estimated future growth |
|---|---|---|---|---|---|
| Dalmeny (house) | 9% | 8% | 2% | 1% | High |
| Armidale (house) | 10% | 2% | 4% | 9% | Medium |
| Penrith (unit) | 7% | 4% | 12% | 9% | Low |
| Penrith (unit) | 7% | 4% | 12% | 9% | Low |

The long-term total return in Dalmeny is higher than in recent years, so some capital growth or rises in rent can be expected. The reverse is true in Harry and Jen's other investment areas, which indicates that this is less likely. The rental yield in Dalmeny is rising, which means that prices rather than rents may be on the move there, while the data is inconclusive for Penrith units. As unit sales trends are falling in Penrith, the data indicates that rents may be on the rise and this is confirmed by their lower value compared with nearby areas.

## Table 9.14: relative potential for rent or capital growth

| Suburb | Long-term total return | Recent total return | Which return is higher? | Capital growth and rental return | Sales trend: falling or rising | Rents compared with nearby areas |
|---|---|---|---|---|---|---|
| Dalmeny (house) | 13% | 6% | Long term | Yield rising | Steady | Higher |
| Armidale (house) | 8% | 14% | Recent | Yield falling | Rising | Higher |
| Penrith (unit) | 13% | 16% | Recent | Yield steady | Falling | Lower |
| Penrith (unit) | 13% | 16% | Recent | Yield steady | Falling | Lower |

From their assessment, Harry and Jen realise that their Penrith units should be retained and that the Armidale house should be sold, as further growth is unlikely in the near future. Dalmeny looks as though there could be significant growth in the next few years, so they decide to hold onto that investment for a while. They use sales and listing data watch lists for all their investments and, having decided to buy inner-city units for the high rental returns, start to maintain watch lists for selected inner suburbs in Sydney and Melbourne.

By keeping track of the performance of their current investments and looking out for potential areas to purchase in Harry and Jen will know when to put each property on the market to get the best price. They will also know when high rental yield opportunities show up on their radar. In this way, Harry and Jen will be able to continue developing their portfolio throughout their retirement, improving their income and lifestyle, and enjoying successfully investing in property as a result.

✦ ✦ ✦

This book has been intended to explain more about the housing market, its nature and how to use the forces that drive it to your advantage than any other property investment book. Its purpose is also to empower you to make the best decisions for your investments, whether buying or selling, no matter what your objectives are.

No matter what stage of the property investment process you are at, or what your personal experience has been, the tools and techniques in this book can work for you. They have been developed over years of testing by professional investors, and are designed to put you into the mind of renters, buyers and sellers, so that you can predict where the market is going and understand why.

If you do not know where you are going, any road will take you there. I trust that this book will put you on the road to successful housing investment, and I wish you all the best on your journey.

# Further resources

Today, a great deal of research on the housing market can be easily conducted using the internet. The problem is that online resources, especially privately provided and run websites, can change rapidly and new websites constantly emerge while others disappear. I suggest you use a search engine and type in the keywords in this section — these will lead you to the correct source, and you may even find new sites that were not available at the time of writing.

## E-newsletters

Property e-newsletters can be a useful source of information. The main problem you are likely to face is deciding which are relevant to your goals and which are not. For example, if you are considering investing in mining towns, the Mining Daily Newsletter is essential reading. However, if you are looking at inner-city units, this newsletter is not going to be useful. Even so, it is better not to cull too rigorously. After all, you do not need to do more than quickly glance through the topics to see if they are relevant and, in any case, your goals could change in the future.

Be wary of free newsletters that are fronts for spuikers, sellers' agents and others with hidden agendas. The common feature in such newsletters is a focus on the person, not their credentials, promises of immense wealth with little evidence of how this is to be obtained and offers to attend a free seminar or workshop where all will be revealed.

Many of the following websites that offer e-newsletters also give you access to their Facebook pages, Twitter accounts and blog sites, ensuring that you will never run short of information.

➤ Australian Property Investor magazine <www.apimagazine. com.au>

➤ Domain <www.domain.com.au>

➤ Home Price Guide <www.homepriceguide.com.au>

➤ homesales.com.au <www.homesales.com.au>

➤ Housing Industry Association media releases <http://hia. com.au>

➤ Mining Australia <www.miningaustralia.com.au>

➤ Mortgage Choice <www.mortgagechoice.com.au>

➤ myRPData <www.myrp.com.au>

➤ Residex <www.residex.com.au>

➤ Smart Company <www.smartcompany.com.au>

> ➤ Understand Property <www.understandproperty.com.au>

> ➤ Westpac property market reports <www.westpac.com.au>.

# Housing information providers

Following are some of the main housing information providers:

> ➤ Home Price Guide <www.homepriceguide.com.au>. This website provides free data and paid reports on the housing market.

> ➤ myRPData <www.myrp.com.au>. This website provides free suburb reports and other paid reports on the housing market.

> ➤ Residex <www.residex.com.au>. This website provides free historical and current data and paid reports on the housing market.

> ➤ Understand Property <www.understandproperty.com.au>. This website provides free independent information and advice on the housing market.

# Sales and listings information providers

For information on sales, prices, rents and listings when properties are listed by a real estate agent, the websites with the most listings and visits include the following:

> ➤ Domain <www.domain.com.au>

> ➤ FindMeAHome <www.fmah.com.au>

> ➤ homehound.com.au <www.homehound.com.au>

➤ realestate.com.au <www.realestate.com.au>

➤ realestateview.com.au <www.realestateview.com.au>.

There are also many listing sites for private vendor sales and a number of sites that specialise in divorce settlement sales, deceased estates and mortgagee in possession sales.

# Magazines

Each issue of the following property investment magazines provides a complete set of data showing historical and current housing prices, sales, rents and listings by suburb.

➤ Australian Property Investor

➤ Your Investment Property.

# Organisational resources

## Australian Bureau of Statistics

You can search the ABS website <www.abs.gov.au> by the name, reference number or subject of current and past releases on topics such as Australian demographic statistics, Australian social trends, dwelling unit commencements, building approvals and housing finance.

## Department of Immigration and Citizenship

The department provides regular updates on the number of, countries of origin, ports of arrival and types of visas for overseas arrivals to Australia. This information is free on its website <www.immi.gov.au>.

## Foreign Investment Review Board

The FIRB advises the government on foreign investment policy and its administration, and provides data on the value, location, number and origin of applications for investment in Australian housing in its annual reports. This information can be viewed on its website <www.firb.gov.au>.

## Housing Industry Association

The HIA <http://hia.com.au> provides complete statistics on housing starts and completions. Its regular press releases (which you can subscribe to) also summarise the data of each publication from the ABS on the housing and housing finance market as they are released.

## National Library of Australia

The NLA's website <www.nla.gov.au> gives you access to electronic copies of newspapers, magazines and other periodicals no longer subject to copyright, from which you can gather historical data on house prices and rents back to colonial times.

# Glossary

The terms in this glossary are some that you are likely to come across when researching the housing market or dealing in residential property investment.

**actual rent**   the rent being paid for a property to the owner.

**apartment**   one of several dwellings in a block, usually owned under strata (or company) title.

**appraisal**   property price estimate provided by a real estate agent to a potential vendor.

**asking rent**   the advertised rent for a property.

**asset** anything of monetary value owned by an individual, group or business.

**attributes** features of a property such as bedrooms, bathrooms, garage spaces, decking, pools, gardens, aspect, views, proximity to services and facilities, land area and floor area.

**auction** the process of selling an asset to the highest bidder.

**automated valuation model (AVM)** an electronically generated property valuation.

**average** a calculated central value of a set of numbers.

**body corporate** a legal entity responsible for administration and maintenance of a unit site and its common property areas. It comprises a committee elected by the owners.

**buyer's agent** someone who acts on behalf of a potential buyer, usually for a fee to locate and negotiate a property purchase on their behalf.

**capital gain** the capital growth realised when an asset is sold.

**capital gains tax (CGT)** tax on net capital gains, which is currently half the rate of income tax for properties owned at least one year.

**capital growth** the increase in the value of an asset over time.

**certificate of title** a document that details the specifications, ownership and current plus discharged mortgages on a property.

**common property** the areas of a strata-titled unit site that are under common ownership, such as gardens, driveways and laundries.

**company title** the precursor to strata title. Company titles still exist for some older unit blocks.

**comparative market analysis (CMA)** property price estimate reports provided by an independent third party.

**conveyancing** the process of legally transferring property ownership from one person or business to another.

**days on market** see *time on market.*

**demographics** the size of a population, its composition, development, distribution and change.

**deposit** an initial payment made to secure the lease or purchase of a property before contracts are prepared and exchanged.

**depreciation** the decline in value of an asset over time.

**equity** the percentage of an asset owned outright. This is the current estimated value less any amount owing.

**flat** one of several dwellings in a block usually owned under strata (or company) title.

**flipping** the practice of buying properties off the plan or under market value and selling for a profit before settlement.

**foreclosure** more commonly known as 'mortgagee in possession' in Australia, this is where a mortgagee has exercised their rights under the mortgage and taken ownership of the property from the mortgagor.

**growth** see *capital growth.*

**housing commission** established by state governments in the postwar period to provide affordable housing for low-income families.

**leasing** renting a property under a written agreement.

**lenders mortgage insurance (LMI)** insurance paid by the borrower to protect the lender in the case of a loan default by the borrower.

**listing**   the public advertising of a property for sale.

**loan to value ratio (LVR)**   the ratio of the amount owing on a mortgage to the estimated value of the property.

**low-doc loan**   a mortgage provided to a property buyer whose income is not fully verified by documentary evidence.

**market value**   the highest price that a property is likely to sell for, usually established by agreement between the vendor and the listing agent.

**mean**   also known as the average, the mean is the middle value of a set of numbers.

**median**   the middle number in a set of numbers.

**mortgage**   the transfer of right of ownership by a debtor to a creditor to provide security on a debt, which continues while the debt remains unpaid.

**mortgagee**   the person or organisation to whom a property is mortgaged.

**mortgagee in possession**   where a mortgagee has exercised their rights under the mortgage and taken ownership of the property from the mortgagor. In the US this is known as foreclosure.

**mortgagor**   the person who mortgages a property.

**negative gearing**   when income from a property (usually rent) is not sufficient to cover costs associated with ownership, such as loan repayments, maintenance, rates and management fees, resulting in negative cash flow. The benefit is that the interest on loan repayments for investment properties is tax deductible.

**no-doc loan**   a mortgage provided to a property buyer whose income is not verified.

**off the plan**   purchase of a property before it has been completed or, in some cases, development has been commenced.

**old system title**   the precursor to Torrens Title. Old system title still exists in some older suburbs, and consists of a description of the property and its origins from the original grant or purchase.

**on the market**   properties that are listed for sale.

**positive gearing**   when the income from a property (usually rent) is more than sufficient to cover costs associated with ownership—such as loan repayments, maintenance, rates and management fees—resulting in a net return to the owner.

**private treaty**   a property sale conducted by the vendor and buyer privately.

**property trading**   buying properties under market value and reselling to achieve a profit.

**rent**   the cost of leasing a property paid by the tenant to the owner.

**rental yield**   also called rental rate and rental return, this is the annual return to the owner from an investment expressed as a percentage of the purchase price of the investment.

**repeat sales**   measuring the change in a property's price the next time it is sold.

**residential**   the zoning of land for residential purposes.

**return**   profit made from an investment.

**rural**   zoning that allows owners to use land for the production of crops or stock.

**security**   an asset, usually a property, on which there is a mortgage.

**strata title**   the title system used for units, flats, apartments and some townhouses and villas, which limits title to each individual unit, and places ownership, administration and maintenance of the block's exterior and common property areas under the control of the body corporate.

**subdivision**   an area of land divided into smaller title lots, usually for residential development.

**tenancy**   period of time a property is leased.

**tenant**   person leasing or renting a property.

**time on market**   the period of time taken for a property to sell from its first listing.

**Torrens Title**   the most common system of freehold title used in Australia, which provides a plan showing the location and dimensions of the property.

**total return**   the combination of capital growth and rental return obtained over a period of time.

**townhouse**   a dwelling that is considered to be either a unit or house depending on the title system used — that is, either strata for units or Torrens for houses.

**unit**   one of several dwellings in a block usually owned under strata (or company) title.

**valuation**   a written estimate of a property's worth usually supplied to the lender by a sworn valuer to determine the actual loan to value ratio and whether lenders mortgage insurance is required.

**vendor**   a property owner who places their property on the market.

**vendor discounting**   the difference between the initial listed asking price for a property and the amount for which it is actually sold.

**vendor sale**   a sale conducted by the owner with no real estate agent involvement.

**zoning**   guidelines for land use usually made by local government authorities.

# Index